AN ANATOMY OF REVELATION

Prophetic Visions in the Light of Scientific Research

Boyce M. Bennett

MOREHOUSE PUBLISHING
Harrisburg, PA • Wilton, CT

Editorial Office
Morehouse Publishing
78 Danbury Road
Wilton, CT 06897

Corporate Office
Morehouse Publishing
P.O. Box 1321
Harrisburg, PA 17105

Library of Congress Cataloging-in-Publication Data

Bennett, Boyce M.
     An anatomy of revelation: prophetic visions in the light of scientific research/
Boyce M. Bennett.
          p.   cm.
     Includes bibliographic references.
     ISBN 0-8192-1502-3
     1. Revelation—Psychology. 2. Psychical research—Religious aspects—Christianity.
3. Prophets. 4. Visions. 5. Dreams. 6. Dreams—Religious aspects—Christianity.
7. Prophecy (Christianity) 8. Religion and science—1946- I. Title.
BT127.2.B46   1990   90-31913
220.1′5′019—dc20   CIP

Printed in the United States of America
by
BSC LITHO
Harrisburg, PA 17105

ii

To my daughter, Becky

Contents

Part Four: The Study of Biblical Literature

Illustrations

Preface

This book is written for a particular audience. It is written for Christians who are both religious and educated, both faithful and questioning. It is intended for people who would like to know more about the relationship between their beliefs about the Bible and their beliefs about the modern world in which they live. It is an attempt to help to eliminate what many may feel to be the remaining bits of conflict between faith and reason, between religion and science. It tries to treat both seriously and to take both of them on their own terms. It asserts that truth is truth, and that there may be many languages and vocabularies to express that truth, but they do not contradict each other if they really are expressing what is true. It is not meant to be a book of answers, but a book of questions that provoke the reader into thinking in new ways about old issues.

My own background is both scientific and theological. My university education (B.S.) was in research chemistry, and for a while I was a research chemist. My theological education took place in seminaries (M.Div., S.T.M., Th.D.). My M.Div. thesis in 1953 was entitled "The Moral Implications of Psychosurgery," so my interest in the brain has been long-standing. But in spite of the scientific emphasis in the first three parts of this book, it is not primarily meant for the scientist. It is meant for the layperson who is interested in what science may say that illuminates the interpretation of parts of the Bible.

My original idea for this book first appeared in a somewhat altered form in *Psi and States of Awareness,* edited by Betty Shapin and Lisette Coly.[1] The modified and expanded form appears here with the permission of the editors. It has been thoroughly revised and updated to include the more recent scientific research done in the various pertinent fields.

To write about a subject that requires one to bridge several disciplinary fields is a somewhat lonely task. But once the implications of recent scientific research became clear to me, I felt compelled to see

---

1. Boyce M. Bennett, "Vision and Audition in Biblical Prophecy as Illuminated by Recent Research on Human Consciousness," *Proceedings of an International Conference Held in Paris, France, August 24–26, 1977,* (New York: Parapsychology Foundation, 1978), 101–30.

if that research would actually illuminate specific biblical problems. I believe that it has. I have tried to be careful to avoid giving the impression that it has explained away anything. I do not believe that anything has been explained away. Mystery still remains. It is just that it is located in a slightly different area.

Boyce M. Bennett, Th.D.
The General Theological
Seminary,
New York City, 1990

Introduction

One of the most obvious facts about Christianity is that it takes revelation seriously. Throughout the centuries, Christians have been quite concerned to determine *what* it is that God has revealed to humanity about himself and what implications that revelation would have for human existence.

It is also true that there has been a somewhat lesser interest in studying *how* God has imparted that revelation to humanity. For the majority of Christians, revelation is seen to be intimately tied to the Bible. But there are a number of ways of understanding the Bible, and Christians do not always agree as to how it should be interpreted.

While most Christians would state that they believe the Bible to be the "Word of God," they tend to position themselves along a continuum when it comes to defining what that phrase really means. At one end of the continuum are those who tend to see the Bible as the "words of God," in the sense that God has dictated to the writers as one might dictate to a secretary. In this sense it is a completely divine document that must be accepted at face value to be what God has spoken. At the other end of the continuum are those who would interpret the phrase to mean that the Bible is the "word concerning God" and as such is a completely human document that can be of great benefit to those who study it.[1] There are many way stations in between these two extremes, e.g., "the Bible is a human document which has been divinely inspired."

It is not my intention in this study to reconcile these two opposing extremes or any of the way stations in between. These views have been around for a long time, and I have nothing new to contribute to the old arguments. But in this study I would like to suggest a completely different approach to the understanding of one aspect of revelation, that of vision.

Although various Christians view revelation in the Bible in different ways, the attempt to understand the revelatory process usually goes

---

1. In grammatical terms the first group understands the phrase "the Word of God" to be an objective genitive phrase. The second group understands it to be a subjective genitive phrase.

back to an assertion that this is the word of God and that the study of a written text is as far as one can go.[2]

What is of interest to me, however, is what happens in the minds of those who are involved in God's revelation *before* they ever commit anything to writing. There is not only the question, What is the psychology of revelation, especially as it pertains to prophecy and the visionary experience? but also the question, What is the biology—or physiology—of that revelation? In other words, speaking from a strictly religious perspective, what is the nature of the human mental equipment that God has created to be at his disposal when he wants to reveal himself to humanity through the biblical prophets? Or, to put the question another way, and speaking from a strictly human perspective, What is the nature of the human mental equipment that the authors of prophetic literature had at their disposal when they experienced visions and auditions?

If people are completely unaware of how the human mind works when it undergoes religious experience, they are going to miss some very important insights when they study the written literature that describes that experience. This is especially true in the study of literature that is written in a style unlike most of our modern literature. The Bible certainly qualifies as an example of such literature.

This study leads into a number of strange areas that seem, at first glance, to be at a great distance from the theological question about revelation that has been posed: split-brain research, altered states of consciousness, the psychology of sleep and dreaming, and paranormal phenomena. However, such a study provides a new set of categories that might help us to understand revelation in a clearer way. It is like acquiring a new set of glasses. At first they may be a little unsettling and may make things look quite different, but after we have become accustomed to them, we realize that we are actually seeing things a lot more clearly than we did before.

So this study will, indeed, lead us into some strange paths that, for a time, will seem to have no connection with the theological pursuit. But they *do* have a connection. If modern scientific research is really searching for truth, it is God's truth for which they are searching— whether the individual scientist happens to be aware of it or not. And if the Incarnation is truly the central teaching of Christianity, it has

---

2. For a summary of the rise of the modern critical study of prophecy see Joseph Blenkinsopp, *A History of Prophecy in Israel* (Philadelphia: Westminster Press, 1983), 26–35.

xii

to be taken seriously. The humanity that was taken on by Christ was *real* humanity and not some ethereal substitute. So a study of the nature of that humanity can, indeed, throw light upon the workings of God.

Part One: Physiology

1. Recent Physiological Research on the Human Brain

People think with their brains, but not all cultures have known this. The ancient Hebrews believed that people thought with their hearts. That does not mean that they believed people "thought emotionally." The center of emotion was located elsewhere in Hebrew folk psychology. But the center of thinking was believed to be in the heart. In modern, Western folk psychology, the heart is understood to be the center of love (our hearts "go out" to people; they get "broken"; they "overflow with love"), but this is no more accurate than the ancient Hebrew folk psychology. The rise of scientific investigation over the past few centuries has shown that folk psychology is no longer an adequate way of understanding human beings. People think with their brains.

The brain is a very mysterious organ. It weighs around two and one half to three pounds and looks something like a large walnut with the shell removed. It has been compared in the past to whatever complicated machines were currently in vogue: an abacus, an adding machine, a computer. But such metaphors can be very misleading, since even the most complicated computer comes nowhere near to being as complicated as the human brain.

Brains, like walnuts, are connected in the center by tissue that looks as if it might be holding the two hemispheres together. In the human brain the largest organ of connection is called the *corpus callosum*. It consists of roughly 300 million nerve fibers that connect the two hemispheres. It is primarily the corpus callosum that allows the two hemispheres to communicate with each other.[1]

The upper, wrinkled surface of the brain is called the cerebral cortex, and it appears to divide the brain into two hemispheres. Actually, it would be more accurate to call the two sides "quatraspheres" since the two of them only make up about half of the brain. This cerebral cortex is a relatively thin sheet of tissue that has overgrown in the skull

---

1. See figure 1.

3

Figure 1. The Corpus Callosum

Medial Section

Corpus Callosum

Coronal Section

Corpus Callosum

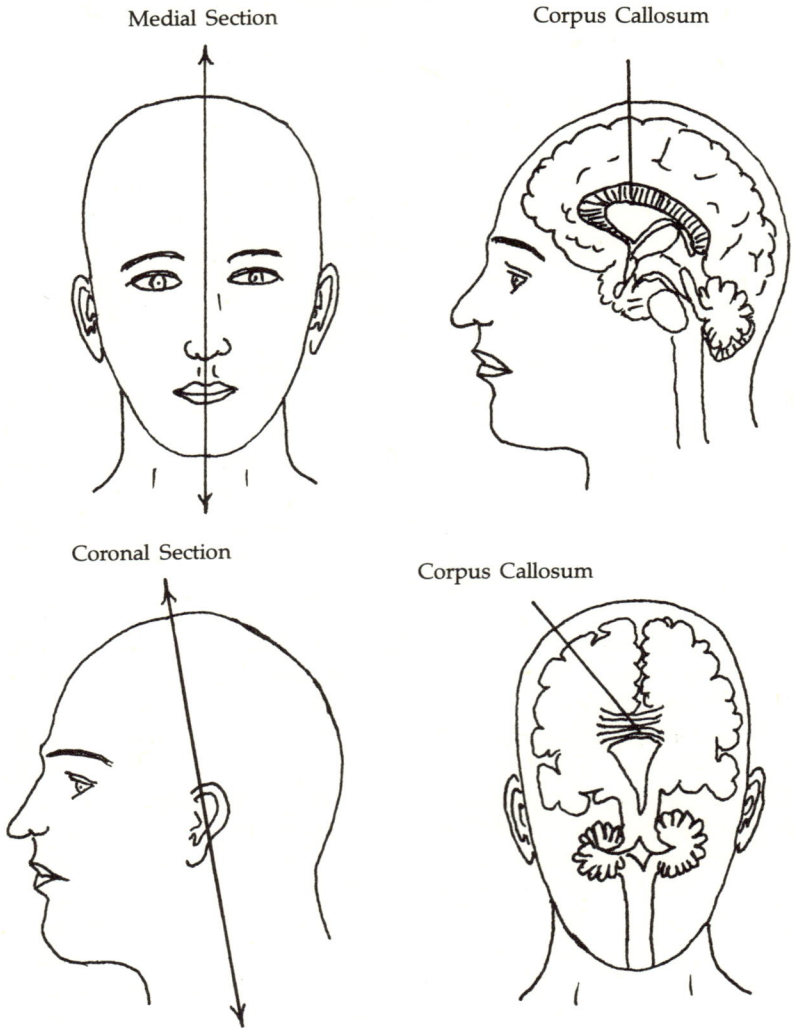

Adapted from Robert H. Lindsay and Donald A. Norman, *Human Information Processing* New York: Academic Press, 1977, 442.

and must wrinkle because of its large size. If it were flattened out, it would cover an area about the size of the surface of a card table.

In the last century or so, greater strides have been made in the study of the human mind than of the human brain. The names of the giants in the science of psychology—Freud, Jung, Adler, etc.—have now become a standard part of the vocabulary of ordinary people. The reasons for this are obvious. Until the last few decades, the study of the physical, living brain has been severely hampered by the inability to study it without surgery. Moral and ethical considerations do not allow such study. Until recently, the only time when something could be learned by direct observation of a living brain was when the brain was injured or when surgery was being performed for other quite legitimate reasons. As a consequence, the science of the psychology of the human mind progressed more rapidly than the science of the physiology of the human brain.

Studies Based upon Injuries

Malfunctions of the brain caused by injuries show provocative evidence without the use of drastic surgery. However, it is almost impossible to interpret such data with any precision because without surgery it is difficult to determine the exact area and extent of the injury. People who have paralysis on the right side of the body because of a stroke are frequently unable to speak coherently (aphasia).[2] This deficit is caused by injury to the speech centers of the left hemisphere. However, such people often utter words or short sentences. When they cannot use more abstract terms, they will often resort to similes, metaphors, or descriptive phrases. But it is only after evidence was uncovered by surgery in recent years that such behavior could be explained and understood.

Stroke victims who are paralyzed on their left side (caused by injury to the right hemisphere) continue to use their left hemisphere in speaking and in interpreting the speech of others, but they are usually unable to comprehend the emotional overtones of the speech of the person talking to them. Since the emotional content is directly connected to the pitch of the voice, and since (as we now know) pitch is a function of the right hemisphere, they are unable to distinguish between anger

---

2. For CAT Scan studies of aphasia, see M.A. Naeser, and J.C. Borod, "Aphasia in Left-Handers: Lesion Site, Lesion Side, and Hemispheric Asymmetries on CT," *Neurology* 36 (April 1986): 471–88; and A. Basso, et al., "Crossed Aphasia: One or More Syndromes?" *Cortex* 21 (March 1985): 25–45.

and elation, between seriousness and joking in the speech of the person to whom they are listening. But this explanation has only recently become possible through information obtained by surgery.

The problem with studying a brain that has been injured is that the sites and extent of the injury are usually fortuitous. As a result, conclusions drawn from a merely external study of an injury must be made very tentatively.

Brain malfunctions that may not have been caused by physical injury are now understood much better because of information gained through surgery. For instance, dyslexia, difficulty with reading, was once thought to be a matter of lack of intelligence.[3] It is now known to be a malfunctioning of the left hemisphere. In dyslexics, both the left and right hemispheres tend to act as if they were right hemispheres. For example, it is possible to teach non-Japanese people with dyslexia to read ideographic Japanese characters because they employ a kind of picture language as opposed to a linear pronunciation of syllables. However, when right-handed Japanese who have learned to read both the pictographic characters and the syllabic characters have strokes on the left side, it is likely that they will have lost the ability to read the syllabic characters but it is just as likely that they will have retained the ability to read the pictorial characters.[4] An explanation for this phenomenon was obtained through a study of the effects of surgery on the brain itself. It is unlikely that it could have been obtained otherwise.

Studies Based upon Invasive Surgical Techniques

Many very surprising things have been learned when the brain has been available for direct study during surgery. Careful ethical and moral distinctions have had to be made between surgery performed for a specific disorder of the brain (disease or injury) and surgery performed strictly for experimentation or brain studies.[5] Because of this distinction, surgeons have had to be careful to keep their motivation clear and to

---

3. Einstein was dyslexic but was obviously not lacking in intelligence. It is a state that usually may not be corrected but may be "worked around."

4. Yamadori, A., Nagashima, I., Iamaki, N., "Ideogram Writing in a Disconnection Syndrome," *Brain Language,* July 1983, 19 (2): 346–56.

5. For those who are unduly upset by having to think about surgery on the human brain, it might be of some help to know that the brain itself has no nerves that give the patient a sensation of pain. Only a local anaesthetic is required to deaden the scalp for such surgery to avoid pain.

make that motivation equally clear to the patient. When the patient undergoes surgery for injury or disease and the doctor wants to study the brain during the operation, the patient must be free either to give or withhold permission for such study.

Committed Areas of the Surface of the Brain

Wilder Penfield, the famous Canadian brain surgeon, has shown that at birth there are certain areas of the brain that are committed to perform specific functions.[6] For example, there are two parallel ridges in the upper midsection of the brain that deal with incoming and outgoing information from various parts of the body.[7] The left hemisphere deals with incoming and outgoing stimulae from the right side of the body; the right hemisphere deals with incoming and outgoing stimulae from the left side of the body. Stimulation of points on the forward ridge by means of a small electric current results in movement of the part of the body on the opposite side that is connected to that site with nerves—without the conscious willing of motion by the patient. This is called the *motor area*. Correspondingly, when points on the other ridge are stimulated, the patient reports receiving a sensation from a specific part of the body on the opposite side—even though there is nothing happening at that place. This is called the *sensory area*.

Other parts of the cerebrum are committed to other functions, e.g., the posterior part of both hemispheres (the occipital lobe) deals with vision, the under portions of the posterior part deal with the recognition of faces, etc.[8] This is true of both hemispheres.

But in the human brain (in contrast to other lower forms of life) there is a great amount of brain tissue in the cortex that is "uncommitted" at birth.[9] In adults it is mostly this uncommitted portion that seems to have areas of specialization that are not duplicated on the other side.

---

6. Wilder Penfield, *The Mystery of the Mind: A Critical Study of Consciousness and the Human Brain*, Princeton University Press, Princeton, N.J., 1975, 19ff.

7. See figure 2.

8. While the underside of the occipital lobes of each hemisphere both deal with the recognition of faces, it is probable that the way in which these areas deal with the recognition of faces is somewhat different. (See the discussion on recognition of faces below.) See also De Renzi, E., "Prosopagnosia in Two Patients with CT Scan Evidence of Damage Confined to the Right Hemisphere," *Neuropsychologia*, 1986, 24 (3): 385-9.

9. Penfield, *The Mystery of the Mind*, 19.

Figure 2. Motor and Sensory Pathways to the Brain

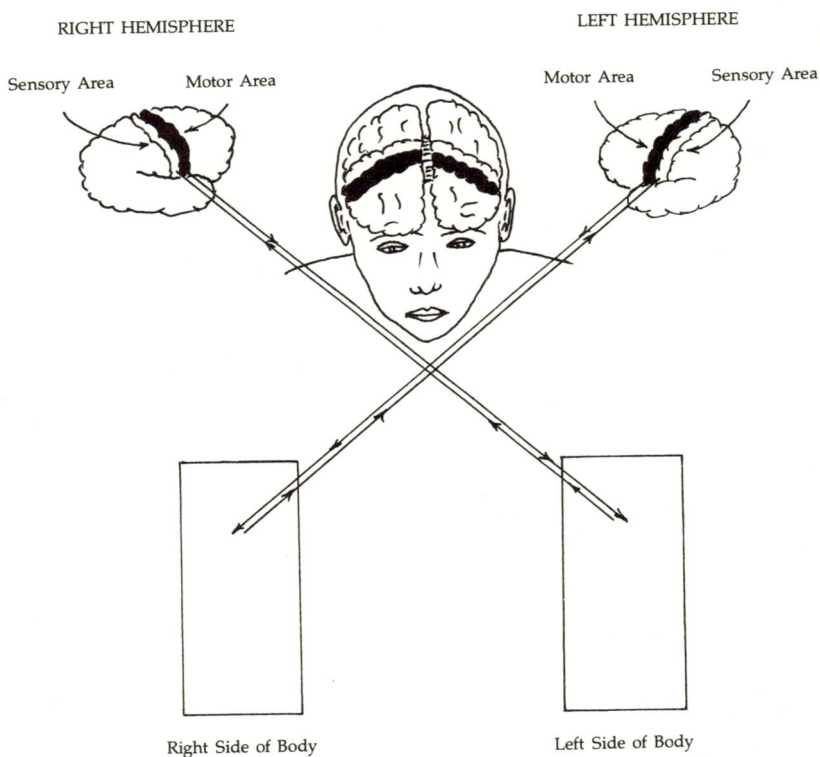

RIGHT HEMISPHERE   LEFT HEMISPHERE

Sensory Area   Motor Area   Motor Area   Sensory Area

Right Side of Body   Left Side of Body

Adapted from Sally P. Springer and Georg Deutsch, *Left Brain, Right Brain,* rev. ed. (New York: W.H. Freeman, 1985), 3.

For example, the Broca's area in the left hemisphere deals with the production of speech, and the Wernicke's area, also in the left hemisphere, deals with the interpretation of speech.[10] The discovery of these functions in the nineteenth century was the first indication that there was any difference in the operation of the two hemispheres. In the first few years of a child's life, when speech is being learned, it is learned in both hemispheres. But as the child matures, the process is more and more confined to the left hemisphere—thus freeing the corresponding area in the right hemisphere for other kinds of work.

Split-Brain Research

While a lot of information has been learned about the brain during surgery performed for other purposes such as that done by Penfield, in 1961 Dr. Roger W. Sperry performed a new operation that was to revolutionize thinking about the brain.[11] His work eventually led to his being awarded the Nobel prize. He began operating on patients who suffered from severe epilepsy in order to relieve them from the severity of their attacks. This experimental surgery turned out to be quite successful for the patient, but it also turned out to throw a great deal of very surprising light on the function of the brain itself.

Since epilepsy usually begins on one side of the brain and then spreads

---

10. A patient who has been injured in the Broca's area has great difficulty speaking but may sing quite easily. When the patient speaks, he or she usually employs faulty grammar, inflects verbs incorrectly, and has difficulty using pronouns, connective words, and complex grammatical constructions. One such patient, when asked about a dental appointment answered, "Yes . . . Monday . . . Dad and Dick . . . Wednesday nine o'clock . . . 10 o'clock . . . doctors . . . and . . . teeth." On the other hand, patients with injuries in the Wernicke's area use speech that is phonetically and grammatically normal, but its meaning is almost impossible to understand. One such patient who was asked to describe a picture showing two boys stealing cookies behind a woman's back said, "Mother is away here working her work to get her better, but when she's looking the two boys looking in the other part. She's working another time." From Seymore S. Kety, "Disorders of the Human Brain," in *The Brain*, W.H. Freeman, New York, 1979, 111–12. See also L. Lund, P.E. Spliid, E. Andersen, M. Bojsen-Miller, "Vowel Perception: A Neuroradiological Localization of the Perception of Vowels in the Human Cortex," *Brain Language*, November 1986, 29 (2): 191–211.
11. For example, see R.W. Sperry, "Lateral Specialization of Cerebral Function in the Surgically Separated Hemispheres," in *The Psychophysiology of Thinking*, ed. F.J. McGuigan and R.A. Schoonover (New York: Academic Press, 1973), 209–29.

over to the other side by means of the corpus callosum, Dr. Sperry decided to cut this connection and thus prohibit the seizure from spreading to the other half of the brain. The technical name for this surgery is *commissurotomy*, but it soon came to be popularized as the *split-brain* operation.

The operation was indeed successful in decreasing the severity of the epilepsy. But the puzzling thing was that even though the surgery was considered to be quite drastic, there was no immediately observable change in the patients. Furthermore, in the beginning there were not even any subjective changes noted by the patients themselves. This seemed to be quite remarkable considering the extreme nature of the surgery they had undergone.

When they were subjected to ordinary psychological tests, there did not seem to be any noticeable change between the results of tests given before and those given after the surgery. Obviously, more sophisticated tests were needed. After surgery, the two hemispheres had been disconnected so that virtually no communication could now take place between them. This separation had to have *some* effect on the patient. New tests had to be devised so that the psychologists could communicate with only one hemisphere at a time. In that way, each hemisphere could be studied separately to see how it functioned when severed from the other hemisphere.

The brain is not the only organ in the body that is paired. A number of other organs are doubled—but in each instance they both perform an identical function. Perhaps the reason for this is that if an injury occurs to one, there is a "backup" system ready to compensate for that loss. But does this assertion apply to the brain as well?

We have known for some time now that the left hemisphere controls the movement of the right side of the body and the right hemisphere controls the movement of the left side of the body. But we have also known since the nineteenth century that most people who are right-handed use their left hemispheres for speech. We knew this because when the left hemisphere was injured by a blow or by a stroke, the person's speech was sometimes seriously affected.[12]

---

12. About 15 percent of left-handers and about 2 percent of right-handers have speech on both sides. Most left-handers have speech on the left side like right-handers, but some do not. Furthermore, if the left hemispheres are damaged in children before they are five or ten years old, they can learn to speak again with the remaining hemisphere after a long period of silence. However, this is much more difficult and frequently impossible in adults.

But what was the function of the right hemisphere? It could not talk and was therefore technically "dumb," but did that mean that it was not smart? The patients whose corpus callosa had been severed by Sperry's surgery now ceased being patients and became subjects of scientific testing.[13]

But the problem remained as to how to communicate with only one hemisphere at a time in order to determine what the functions of that hemisphere might be.

The answer to this problem was that such communication could be done through the eyes.[14] However, that was not as simple as it might seem on the surface. We might think that, if we covered up the right eye, everything that the left eye saw would be communicated to the left hemisphere and vice versa. But this is not the case.

The visual system is constructed so that everything that enters a single eye goes to both hemispheres at once. This is accomplished by the *optic chiasm*. The nerves that are connected to the retina at the back of a single eye divide and go to both hemispheres.[15]

However, the nerves on the left side of the center of the retina of both eyes *do* go only to the left hemisphere and the nerves on the right side of the center go only to the right hemisphere. Note that the lens of the eye reverses all incoming images, so that the right field of vision (anything to the right of the focusing point of sight) will be sent to the left hemisphere and vice versa.

Consequently, if the subjects could keep their eyes focused on a central spot, everything to the right of that spot goes to their left hemisphere, and everything to the left of that spot goes to their right hemisphere. Since the corpus callosum has been severed in these patients, the hemispheres may no longer share information with each other. So, at last, here was a way to send information to one hemisphere without the other hemisphere's being aware of it.

Here is a summary of the general distinctions between the functions

13. By the late 1980s, a little over one hundred patients had undergone this operation.
14. What follows is a fairly complicated explanation of how communication can take place through the eyes with only one hemisphere. If this is not of interest to the reader, it is possible to skip to the section that begins with the result of these tests. See "Type of Thought," below.
15. See figure 3.

Figure 3. The Optic Chiasm

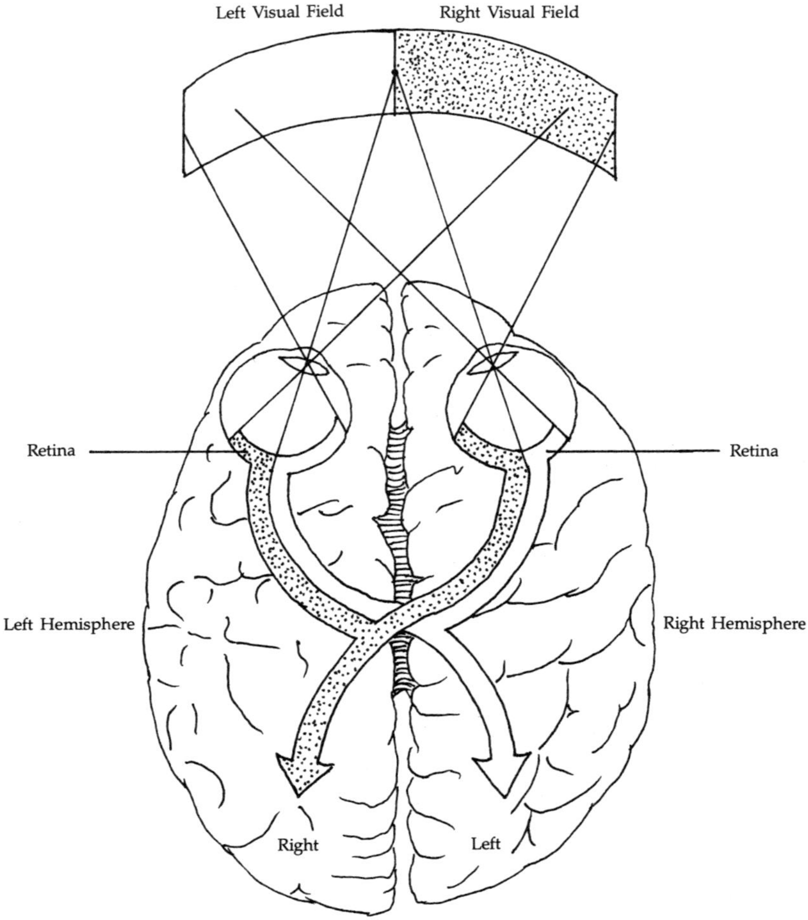

Left Visual Field   Right Visual Field

Retina —   — Retina

Left Hemisphere   Right Hemisphere

Right   Left

Adapted from Sally P. Springer and Georg Deutsch, *Left Brain, Right Brain*, rev. ed. (New York: W.H. Freeman, 1985), 32.

of the left and right hemispheres that have been discovered by communicating with only one hemisphere at a time.[16]

TYPE OF THOUGHT: The left hemisphere uses logical and abstract thought. This hemisphere thinks in a linear, verbal fashion, stringing words together in a specific order in order to arrive at a conclusion. This is usually the kind of thinking people do when they "talk to themselves" in their minds. In contrast to the left hemisphere, the right hemisphere does not think illogically but instead uses analogical thought.[17] This hemisphere uses a lot of visual and verbal imagery in its thinking. It is more interested in what a thing may be *compared to* than what it actually *is*, what a thing is *like* than the precise *definition* of that thing.

TYPE OF REASONING: The left hemisphere uses analytical, linear reasoning. It uses words and numbers rationally and restricts their meanings to a single definition, like specific entries in a dictionary. It thinks verbally and numerically. The right hemisphere uses holistic, nonlinear reasoning. It has an intuitive use of visual and verbal imagery. It thinks in poetic symbols; it uses puns and *double entendre*. It is more like Roget's thesaurus than Webster's dictionary.

NAMES AND FACES: The left hemisphere is better at remembering names than recognizing faces. It can identify faces only by concluding logically that this is a particular person (because the person is, for example, "female, blonde, and wearing glasses"). The right hemisphere recognizes faces, not by logic, but by actually knowing what a person *looks like* from memory.[18]

---

16. These general statements about the functions of the hemispheres have to be updated and refined continually as new research gives specific nuance to each statement.

17. M.S. Gazzaniga, et al., "Profiles of Right Hemisphere Language and Speech Following Brain Bisection," *Brain Language*, July 1984, 22 (2): 206–20; also R. Joseph, "The Neuropsychology of Development Hemispheric Laterality, Limbic Language, and the Origin of Thought," *Journal of Clinical Psychology*, January 1982, 38 (1): 4–33; J.J. Sidtis, et al., "Variability in Right Hemisphere Language Function after Callosal Section: Evidence for a Continuum of Generative Capacity," *Journal of Neuroscience*, March 1981, 1 (3): 323–31; V.W. Henderson, et al., "CT Criteria of Hemisphere Asymmetry Fail to Predict Language Laterality," *Neurology*, August 1984, 34 (8): 1086–89.

18. M.S. Gazzaniga, and C.S. Smylie, "Facial Recognition and Brain Asymmetries: Clues to Underlying Mechanisms," *Annals of Neurology*, May 1983, 13 (5): 536–40.

MUSIC: The left hemisphere can analyze music intellectually but when it tries to sing a tune, the pitch is monotone. This hemisphere can discuss the *meaning* that the words in a song intend to convey, even recite the words in an attempt to sing, but the tune is monotone. The right hemisphere is able to sing songs using the correct pitch and the right words but is unable to discuss the *meaning* that the words in the song are meant to convey.[19]

TIME: The left hemisphere can keep track of the passage of time. It can learn Morse code and keep time in music. The right hemisphere does not have a sense of time. It can neither learn Morse code nor keep time in music.

SPACE: The left hemisphere is spatially "naive." It cannot copy correctly a line drawing because it cannot get the spatial arrangement of the lines correct. It cannot even copy words correctly, but it can read the words. (It has the speaking and reading vocabulary of an adult.) It cannot recognize ordinary objects by touch alone because this skill involves the use of spatial ability. The right hemisphere can copy line drawings or words, but it has difficulty reading some words. Even though it cannot speak, the right hemisphere has the reading vocabulary of a teenager and the syntactical ability of a five- or six-year-old.[20] It can recognize ordinary objects by touch alone because of its spatial expertise.

---

19. The left hemisphere is able to sing "Mary had a little lamb," but it will be sung in a monotone. That hemisphere is also able to discuss the meaning that the words of the song were meant to convey. The right hemisphere can sing "Mary had a little lamb" in proper pitch and with the proper words, but it is unable to discuss the nature of the small, white, furry animal that Mary had in her possession.

20. In the first few years of life, children learn everything on both sides of their brains. Then a white, fatty substance begins to form a sheath around the nerve fibers of the corpus callosum (almost as if wires were being insulated) until that process is complete. During these years the hemispheres specialize more and more until finally the specialization is complete a few years before adolescence. The hemisphere that no longer specializes in speech (the right hemisphere) does not completely forget the vocabulary it has learned earlier, but it can no longer communicate in speech. It does, however, recognize simple written words and simple written commands. See R. Joseph et al., "Two Brains, One Child: Interhemispheric Information Transfer Deficits and Confabulatory Responding in Children Aged 4, 7, 10," *Cortex*, September 1984, 20 (3): 317–31; D.S. O'Leary, "A Developmental Study of Interhemispheric Transfer in Children Aged Five to Ten," *Child Development*, September 1980, 51 (3): 743–50.

MOOD: The left hemisphere seems to be related to happiness. When the opposite hemisphere is anaesthetized, the person has euphoria, smiles, laughs, sometimes with the intensity of maniacal behavior. The right hemisphere seems to be related to depression. When the opposite hemisphere is anaesthetized, the person exhibits depression, feelings of guilt, indignity, and anxiety about the future.[21]

CONSCIOUSNESS: People are normally aware of the content of their thinking in the left hemisphere. Everyone spends many hours each day consciously discussing things in their minds. However, they are normally unaware of the content of their thinking in the right hemisphere. They become aware of that kind of thinking when, for example, they dream.[22]

PRIMARY AND SECONDARY PROCESS: The left hemisphere deals in what Freud called *Secondary Process*—the logical thought people use when they talk to themselves silently. The right hemisphere deals in *Primary Process*—the kind of thinking evident in the thinking of small children and in dreams.

There seems to be a kind of "suspicion" that exists between the two hemispheres in the patients examined. It is as if each hemisphere mistrusts the other hemisphere and discounts the way in which it operates. Neither hemisphere fully understands the other because each operates so differently.

If the information obtained from split-brain patients has been interpreted accurately, this means that the cerebral cortex does not duplicate everything on both sides but that one hemisphere is specialized for one kind of thinking and the other hemisphere for another kind of thinking. As a consequence of this lateralized specialization, there is more total space on the human cortex for specific functions. If every thinking function does not have to be duplicated, that means that there

21. H. Terzian, "Behavioral and EEG Effects of Intracarotid Sodium Amytal Injection," *Acta Neurochirurgia (Wein)* 12 (1964): 230-39. For more recent studies based upon CAT scan procedures, see R.G. Robinson, et al., "Mood Disorders in Left-Handed Stroke Patients," *American Journal of Psychiatry*, December 1985, 142 (12): 1424-29.
22. M.S. Gazzaniga, J.E. LeDoux, and D.H. Wilson, "Language, Praxis, and the Right Hemisphere: Clues to Some Mechanisms of Consciousness," *Neurology*, December 1977, 27 (12): 1144-47; D.M. Armstrong, "Three Types of Consciousness [Commentary]," *Ciba Foundation Symposium*, 1979, (69): 235-53.

is twice as much space available for thinking on the cortex. It expands the capability of human thought by a factor of two!

Facts like these have eventually led Sperry and his associates to believe that there are two minds in all of us. The right hemisphere thinks in Primary Process (Mode I) terms; the left hemisphere thinks in Secondary Process (Mode II) terms. Bimodal consciousness is a part of normal human mental equipment.[23] Split-brain surgery removes one of those minds from any access to the consciousness of the patient.

The assertion that we have two minds is hard to believe. We do not feel as if we had two minds. But all of us have had to give up "obvious" truths as we mature and learn more about ourselves and our world. The earth is not flat, even though it looks that way. Neither is the earth the center of the universe, even though it serves quite well as the center of *our* universe. We have even had to give up the notion that matter could never be destroyed but merely changed in its chemical composition; atomic research has compelled all of us to live without such assumptions.

While the information discussed here is of great interest to those who study the physiology of the brain, some of it is of equally great interest to those who want to know if this new knowledge can shed any light upon the working of the minds of biblical prophets and, as a result, upon prophetic literature itself.

The right hemisphere uses a certain kind of specialized thinking. It specializes in Primary Process thought; in analogical, holistic, nonlinear reasoning; in an intuitive use of visual and verbal imagery; in poetic symbols, puns, and *double entendre.* A sizeable portion of prophetic literature could easily be described in these terms. Such a category seems to have not only a logical rationale but, perhaps, even some physiological basis.

The way the brain is constructed obviously influences the way we see reality. The concept of bimodal consciousness that was developed through split-brain research seems to give a certain "legitimacy" to analogical thinking because one hemisphere of the brain is thought to specialize in that kind of thinking.

Bimodal consciousness seems to be a normal part of human mental equipment, even though many people are subjectively unaware of this

---

23. P.A. Anninos, P. Argyrakis, and A. Skouras, "A Computer Model for Learning Processes and the Role of the Cerebral Commissures," *Biological Cybernetics*, 1984, 50 (5): 329–36.

fact. People only become aware of the duality of their consciousness when their state of consciousness has been altered in some way. Perhaps the concept of bimodal consciousness can illuminate our understanding of prophetic mentality.

Studies Based upon Noninvasive Procedures

Even though a great deal of information can be obtained by examining the living human brain during surgery, such exploration can only be done when the surgery is being performed for other serious and legitimate reasons. Recent scientific equipment, however, has made such study possible without the invasion of the brain by surgical methods.[24] The results of such investigations are indeed amazing.

One of the first noninvasive techniques used to study the brain was the electroencephalograph (EEG). It had been known since 1929 that the brain sends out electromagnetic waves of different frequencies and that these waves can be recorded by attaching electrodes at various places on the scalp. It is as if the brain were a city that had several radio stations, each broadcasting on different frequencies, and each broadcasting all the time. At certain times each station turns up the amplitude (volume) for a period and then turns it down again.

When the brain is in intense activity (wide-awake, concentrated thought), it sends out waves from a frequency of 14 cycles per second to many times that amount. This range has been called *beta* waves.

If the brain is at rest (frequently with the eyes closed) and not accomplishing active thought, it sends out waves from a frequency of 8 to 13 cycles per second. This range has been given the designation of *alpha* waves.

---

24. In addition to the X rays, which have been available since the end of the nineteenth century, we now have such procedures as pneumoenephalography (which can show the condition of the ventricles, or cavities of the brain); cerebral angiography (which uses dye to make the blood vessels of the brain visible to X rays); CAT scan (which takes X rays from different angles to photograph accurate cross sections of the brain); electroencephalography (which measures the electrical fields near the surface of the brain); oxygen and glucose consumption (which show on a cathode ray tube the particular areas of the brain that are working hardest at that moment); histoflourescence and immuno-flourescence (which measure the effects of chemical transmitters on individual neurons). As further research continues, more and more procedures are being devised to study the brain without surgery.

As the subject begins to descend into sleep, brain waves of a frequency of between 4 and 8 cycles per second are produced. This range is called *theta* waves.

In deep sleep, brain waves of 0.5 to 3 cycles per second may be recorded. These waves are called *delta* waves.[25]

Readings of brain waves in conscious patients have been used for many years to help diagnose abnormalities in the brain. But it is only in the past few decades that scientists have begun to study the brain wave patterns of normal subjects during sleep. When electrodes are attached to various parts of the head and subjects are asked to sleep all night with them in place, continuous recordings of these waves may be made. Many surprising things have been discovered using this method.

At the beginning of the night when the subjects get in bed, close their eyes, and begin to relax, the frequencies start to shift from active thinking beta waves to relaxed alpha waves. Consciousness begins to disappear at the lower end of the alpha range and theta waves appear. Finally, deep sleep arrives and produces the slow-moving delta waves.[26]

However, this descent into deep sleep does not last throughout the night. It has been shown that there is a pattern of brain wave activity that repeats itself approximately every hour and a half. After delta waves are produced in deep sleep, the frequency gradually increases until it comes into the theta range for a period of time and then decreases back into the delta range during the next cycle. The first cycle is characterized by a very deep descent into the lowest frequency range. However, the second cycle does not drop so deeply, and the following cycles are progressively less and less deep. Accordingly, the amount of time spent in the theta portion of the cycle increases from about 9 or 10 minutes at the beginning of the night to four or five times that amount before waking in the morning.

Delicate equipment placed upon the eyes during these experiments records the movement of the eyes during sleep. Scientists noticed that every time a cycle went from delta to theta, the subjects' eyes would change from slow, uncoordinated movement in the delta period to rapid, coordinated movement during the theta period. When subjects were awakened during the rapid eye movement, they usually reported that they had been dreaming. When subjects were awakened during

25. Kenneth A. Kooi, *Fundamentals of Electroencephalography*, Harper & Row, New York, 1971.
26. See figure 4, upper half.

Figure 4. EEG Patterns

SLEEP CYCLES

Alpha

Stages of Sleep

Time in Hours

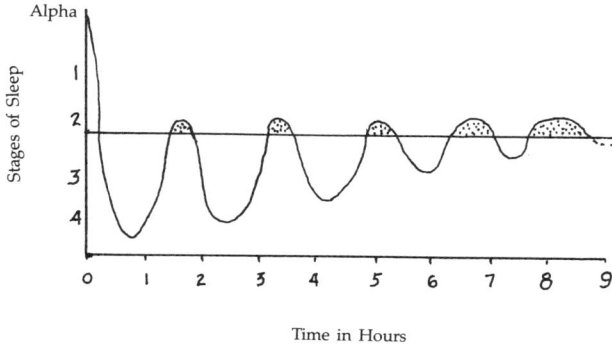

WAKING CYCLES   SLEEP CYCLES

Secondary Process Thought

Primary
Process
Thought

Secondary Process Thought

Time in Hours

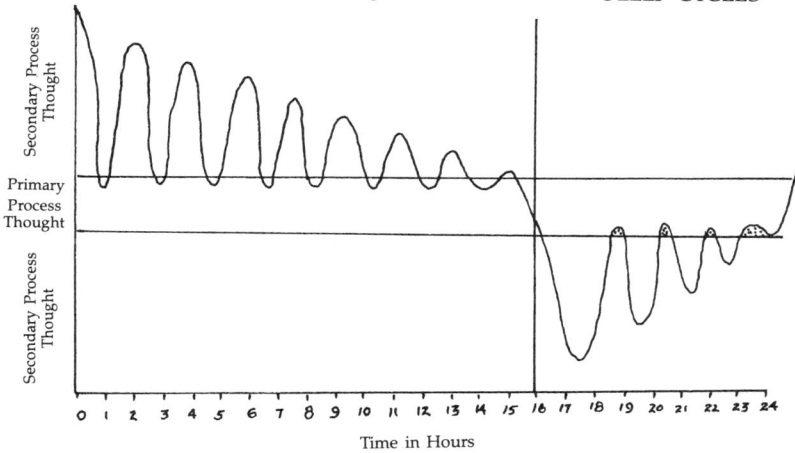

Adapted from Richard M. Jones, *The New Psychology of Dreaming* (New York: Grune and Stratton, 1970), 37.

the delta periods, they did not report dreaming as such, but they reported that they had been mulling over problems that they faced during the day. The sleep researchers began calling the rapid eye movement (REM) periods "dreaming sleep," while they called the slow eye movement (SEM) periods "thinking sleep." The amazing thing is that there seems to be no time during sleep when the brain is not at work.

Using electrodes to study the brain in this fashion is a relatively crude method of exploration. It is something like taking a stethoscope into a room that contains a large "mainframe" computer in order to determine how that computer works. One can listen to the various whirs and hums that are produced by this computer in various places at different times, but the amount of information that can be obtained in this way must surely be limited.

In spite of the crudeness of this method, some surprising information has been obtained. It is now known that, during the waking hours, the hour and a half cycle that was present during sleep continues to operate. The difference is that, in contrast to the deep delta "troughs" during sleep, there are high beta "peaks" at 90-minute intervals throughout the waking period. These alternate with low alpha "troughs." The beta periods correspond with intense mental concentration; the alpha periods correspond with more relaxed day-dreaming states.[27]

One of the most intriguing sections of this brain wave series of cycles is the transition period between waking and sleeping. It is during the gradual descent between waking and sleeping that subjects experience "mini-dreams"; brief images that are more like film clips or short slide shows than the full length movies that are characteristic of REM dreams. These images are called *hypnagogic* when they are experienced on the way toward sleep and *hypnopompic* when they are experienced on the way toward wakefulness. Both hypnagogic and hypnopompic dreams have similar characteristics, so we will confine ourselves to the term *hypnagogic*.

The word *hypnagogic* was coined by Maury in 1848.[28] A hypnagogic image is to be distinguished from an image that is intentionally imagined. Hypnagogic images seem to "come to" the dreamer rather than appear as the result of conscious imagination. Hypnagogic visions are usually

---

27. See figure 4, lower half.
28. Ian Oswald, "Drowsy Dreams are Micro Dreams," *The New World of Dreams*, ed. Ralph L. Woods, and Herbert B. Greenhouse, New York: Macmillan, 1974, 314.

visual, less frequently auditory, and sometimes kinesthetic or olfactory.[29] In contrast to REM dreaming, the eyes move slowly when hypnagogic images appear.

Usually in REM dreaming the dream has visual continuity and resembles a rather bizarre movie. At least some of the hypnagogic experiences are reported not to have that kind of continuity. They seem to be more like still shots of film clips. The content can be integrated in an ideational or conceptual way rather than by visual continuity.[30]

Since hypnagogic images are experienced at the beginning of sleep, they are usually forgotten by the time morning has come. However, if subjects are wakened at the beginning of the period of sleep because the readings of the electroencephalograph indicate that they are having such images, they can describe the images to the experimenter. These experiences are frequently described as being vivid, but the dreamers are usually minimally involved in the scene itself. The subjects take a role as passive spectator more than the role of the main character in a story (as in a REM dream). Sometimes such images remain for a few moments after the subjects are fully awake. One student dreamed that he saw a spider, and he saw it for a few moments after he awoke. One student saw an angel, which remained some moments after awaking.[31]

In this chapter, the brain has been described in terms of physiology. Information obtained from brain surgery has led to the concept of bimodal consciousness. Both REM dreams and hypnagogic dreams use Mode I thought, and both have been studied through noninvasive techniques.

One of the characteristics of seeing a hypnagogic image is that it seems to "come to" the subject from the outside; it does not seem to be the product of intentional imagination. It is experienced as something that

29. David Foulkes has reported that hypnagogic experiences are primarily visual. Auditory and kinesthetic imagery were present in roughly one quarter of hypnagogic experiences. Affect seems to be neither as frequent or as intense in hypnagogic experiences as emotion in REM dreams. David Foulkes, *The Psychology of Sleep*, Charles Scribner's Sons, New York, 1966, 125; David Foulkes, "How Do Hypnagogic Dreams Differ from REM Dreams?" in *New World of Dreams*, ed. Woods and Greenhouse. 319.
30. Foulkes, *Psychology of Sleep*, 125.
31. Ian Oswald, "Drowsy Dreams are Micro Dreams," in *New World of Dreams*, ed. Woods and Greenhouse, 314.

is "happening to" the recipient, not something that is "being caused by" the recipient. The visionary acts as a *passive* spectator of the vision, not an imaginative playwright who is creating a production by willing it to exist.[32] This is an important distinction and contributes to the view, on the part of the visionary, that the hypnagogic vision borders on "objective reality," no matter how bizarre that image is.[33] If some prophetic visions are hypnagogic in nature, we can understand why the prophets see the visions as arising outside themselves. Prophets usually say, "Thus says the Lord . . . ," rather than, "When I was thinking the other day, it seemed to me that . . ."

People dream both REM and hypnagogic dreams, and that statement is a statement about the physiology of the brain. As fascinating as a *physiological* study of the human brain may be, there are other, equally interesting ways of thinking about the work of the brain. It can be studied from a *psychological* point of view as well.

A psychological study looks, not at the fact that people dream, but at the dreams themselves. It tries to understand the purpose and meaning of dreams. Such a study may also help to understand the minds of the biblical prophets.

---

32. See B.D. Napier, s.v. "vision," *Interpreter's Dictionary of the Bible* (1962) for the various uses of the term *vision* in the Old Testament.
33. Some atheists will tend to see biblical visions as coming totally from the subject and therefore from the "inside." Some theists will tend to see it as coming totally from God and therefore from the "outside." Other theists will tend to see it as a genuinely human experience that may be used by God for his own purposes. Readers may find themselves at various points between the two extremes.

Part Two: Psychology

2. Psychological Studies of Dreaming

Dreams as Problem Solvers

Much research has gone into the study of the dreaming state. To ask the question, What is the purpose of dreaming? is to show what a complicated question that is. It is similar to asking the question, What is the purpose of conscious thought? There are many purposes and many reasons for thought. Consequently, there is a great deal of disagreement concerning the basic purpose of dreams. However, there is at least one common thread that runs throughout many of the major theories. Some dreams (as well as some conscious, waking thoughts) seem to be directed toward the solving of *problems* that confront the dreamer. This function seems to be true of REM dreams as well as the shorter hypnagogic dreams.

If it is true that REM and hypnagogic dreaming seem to be involved more with the right than with the left hemisphere, and if the new findings of split-brain research continue to hold up, then it is to be expected that the problem solving would be done in symbolic rather than abstract, logical forms.

For example, William Dement conducted an experiment at Stanford University in which students were instructed to look at a particular brain-teasing problem for only fifteen minutes before going to bed; then, if it had not been solved, they were to spend fifteen more minutes trying to solve it the next morning. They were also to record any dreams they had during the night. Out of the five hundred students involved in the experiment, many were unable to solve the problem, and only a few were helped in that solution by examining their dreams. It is possible that many of them were not very highly motivated to solve the problem, but the few who were helped by their dreams served as quite remarkable examples of the dream process as a problem solver. One of the brain-teasers was as follows:

The letters O, T, T, F, F, . . . form the start of an infinite sequence. What is the rule for determining any or all successive letters?

According to your rule what are the next two letters of the sequence?

The answer is that the letters are the first letters of the words *one, two, three, four, five* . . . so the next two letters are "S (six) and S (seven)!"[1]

One student dreamed the following dream:

> I was standing in an art gallery looking at the paintings on the wall. As I walked down the hall, I began to count the paintings— one, two, three, four, five. But as I came to the sixth and seventh, the paintings had been ripped from their frames! I stared at the empty frames with a peculiar feeling that some mystery was about to be solved. Suddenly I realized that the sixth and seventh spaces were the solution to the problem.[2]

Another brain teaser went as follows: "Consider these letters: H, I, J, K, L, M, N, O. The solution to this problem is one word. Find that word."[3] The solution is the word *water*. The sequence is "H to O," or, as a chemical formula, H_2O, the formula for water.

One student seems to have dreamed the answer in several forms but still did not recognize it as the answer.

> I had several dreams, all of which had *water* in them somewhere. In one dream I was hunting for sharks. In another I was riding waves at the ocean. In another I was confronted by a barracuda while skin diving. In another dream it was raining quite heavily. In another I was sailing into the wind.[4]

In the above case, however, the student thought he had solved the brain teaser before going to bed. He had decided that the answer ought to be the word *alphabet*! It was incorrect, and perhaps his unconscious mind was trying to correct it.

Many examples of this kind of problem-solving dream are well known. The chemist Kekulé had been trying for a long time to figure out how a molecule with six carbon atoms and twelve hydrogen atoms could be pictured on paper without having two valences left over. (All valences must be attached to other atoms in stable compounds.) He

---

1. Christopher Evans, *Landscapes of the Night: How and Why We Dream* (New York: Viking Press, 1983), 230ff.
2. Ibid., 232.
3. Ibid., 231.
4. Ibid., 232.

had been unable to solve this particular problem until he had a dream during a reverie state (a hypnagogic dream) that took the form of a snake swallowing its own tail. All of a sudden he awoke and realized he had to put the string of atoms together in the form of a circle, and thus the symbol of the benzine ring was invented.[5]

When I first began to study hemisphere specialization, I thought about it constantly during the day in an almost obsessive fashion. After a long day of concentrated thought, I went to sleep and had a dream that showed that my right hemisphere also was trying to figure it all out. But it was trying to figure it out in its own vocabulary and in its own inimitable style.

I dreamed that I was standing before a post office, trying to figure out how post offices worked. All of a sudden it came to me. The letters were kept in the room on the left and the packages were kept in the room on the right.

When I awoke, I realized that I was expressing in concrete terms some very abstract ideas. In the dream I was studying a post office, a center of communication (the brain). I realized with my right hemisphere that linear thought (letters) took place in the left room (hemisphere) while three-dimensional pictorial thought (packages) took place in the room on the right. It was something like a "eureka" experience for me.

One of the passages in the Acts of the Apostles sounds, in its present form in the text, like a hypnagogic, problem-solving experience. Peter had been concerned for some time about whether it was right to allow Gentiles in the new Christian Church. It had been occupying his mind for a long time, and it was a momentous decision. The story is as follows:

The next day, as they were on their journey and coming near the city, Peter went up on the housetop to pray, about the sixth hour [around noon]. And he became hungry and desired something to eat; but while they were preparing it, he fell into a trance [the

---

5. "I turned my chair to the fire and dozed. Again the atoms were gamboling before my eyes. This time the smaller groups kept modestly to the background. My mental eye, rendered more acute by repeated visions of this kind, could not distinguish larger structures . . . all twining and twisting in a snakelike motion. But look! What was that? One of the snakes had seized hold of its own tail, and the form whirled mockingly before my eyes." August Kekulé, 1890, quoted in *Brain Mind Bulletin* (July 26, 1986): 2.

reverie of hypnagogic sleep?] and saw the heaven opened, and something descending, like a great sheet, let down by four corners upon the earth. In it were all kinds of animals and reptiles and birds of the air [the visual image]. And there came a voice to him, "Rise, Peter; kill and eat" [an auditory element]. But Peter said, "No, Lord; for I have never eaten anything that is common or unclean." And the voice came to him again a second time, "What God has cleansed, you must not call common." This happened three times, and the thing was taken up at once to heaven. (Acts 10:9ff., RSV)

If hypnagogic images are sometimes used as problem solvers, this could be seen as contributing to the solution that Peter was trying to find. It was forbidden by Jewish ritual law for Jews and Gentiles to associate with each other under certain conditions; Gentiles were ritually "unclean." It was also against Jewish law for a Jew to eat anything ritually "unclean." (Peter's vision implies that to allow Gentiles into the Church was "to incorporate," "to put into the body" of the Church, the ritually unclean Gentile.) But the problem is solved if God himself cleanses the unclean thing. In other words, it is possible to allow Gentiles into the Church if they have been cleansed by God.

Note carefully that the question under investigation is not, Did God answer this problem for Peter? Nor is it, Did Peter answer this problem for himself? The question is, What is the nature of the human mental equipment that God has at his disposal when he wants to reveal himself? Or conversely, What is the nature of the mental equipment the people have at their disposal when they try to solve problems in an altered state of consciousness that were insoluble in their ordinary state of consciousness? Again, some atheists may say that this is the work of Peter's own mind; some theists may say that this is an example of God's use of miracle to reveal his will. Other theists may say that God is using Peter's own mind to reveal God's will in a completely natural and human way. None of these assertions can be proved on its own merits.

It is probable that in most of the cases discussed above, the intensity of the frustration caused by not being able to solve the problem in a waking and logical way has encouraged the dreaming mechanism to "kick in" in an altered state of consciousness so that the problem could be solved *ana*logically (as opposed to logically).

Dreams as Attempts to Resolve Emotional Conflict

Montague Ullman gives a very helpful summary of what he sees dreams to be.[6] Dreams are concerned primarily with unfinished emotional business, or in psychiatric terms, "areas of unresolved conflict." A seemingly unimportant event during the day that was hardly given full attention at the time may open up an area of conflict that is worked on in the form of a dream during the night. The incident that actually triggered the dream sometimes appears in the dream and is known as *day residue*.[7] It is frequently something that occurs in the day prior to the dream or sometimes somewhat earlier than that.

The individual parts of the dream are made up of several elements. The dreamer looks back over his or her past life and gathers together incidents that are historically related to the unresolved conflict or are similar to it so that they may shed any light upon the problem under consideration.

Once the unresolved emotional business is decided upon, once the "subject of conversation" is determined, the dreamer is ready to construct the dream. Using the various memories that seem to be related to the conflict or are similar to it, the dreamer constructs the dream in the language that is understood by the right hemisphere: analogical, pictorial, poetic, symbolic imagery. (It is to be noted that the use of such symbols is not necessarily an attempt to disguise the content of the dream from the dreamer—as Freud believed—but is a genuine desire to communicate with the dreamer in the only language that this part of the brain understands.)[8]

The resulting dream is a drama that is written by the dreamer to explore the various implications of the situation in analogical terms and allows an interplay between the character hang-ups (defense mechanisms) and the resources that can be used for a resolution of the conflict.

6. Montague Ullman, Stanley Krippner, and Alan Vaughan, *Dream Telepathy*, New York: (Macmillan, 1973), 222ff.

7. A fascinating experiment on day residue was conducted by Howard Roffwarg and his associates in 1978. Nine subjects were required to wear goggles over a stated period of time, which made them see everything in shades of red throughout the day. Their dreams showed that everything that appeared in red in the dream was actually day residue, and the rest of the material was clearly derived from memories of earlier experiences. These results suggested that there is "some complicated interaction between recent experience and memory." Jonathan Winson, *Brain and Psyche*, Garden City: Anchor Press, Doubleday, 1985, 210ff.

8. This is not to say that people do not sometimes try to hide some things from their conscious selves. It is merely to assert that dream symbolism is not meant, in every case, to disguise the real meaning but, on the contrary, to *communicate* in the analogical language of the right hemisphere.

The mood, or feeling, of the setting of the dream is important because it gives a clue to the nature of the problem under discussion in the dream. The dream continues to develop into a play that explores analogically the various ramifications of the conflict and the possibilities of its resolution.

If the conscious mind is to make any constructive use of a dream, it must be willing to treat the dream seriously, thinking deeply about the themes presented in the dream, puzzling over the symbolic elements, the puns, and the metaphors used in the script of the dream, no matter how embarrassing or how surrealistic they may seem to the waking mind. It is not necessary to employ the help of an expert in dream interpretation because the symbols are the invention of the dreamer; they are not taken from some standard "dream book."

If enough work is done in this vein, it is eventually possible to write a paragraph in *prose* describing the problem that has been under discussion in the dream in *poetic,* metaphorical form. This is the primary way in which the left hemisphere understands what is being considered by the right hemisphere. It requires serious analytical thinking.

The Twilight Zone Between Waking and Sleeping

In the past few decades a number of scientists have become interested in studying the brains and the minds of people in religious communities that specialize in mental prayer of various types. The nomenclature of the different kinds of prayer is different for each religious tradition, and as a consequence, one must define very carefully the terms under discussion to avoid complete confusion.

Most of the study of the scientists has been concerned with Zen meditation, Yoga, Christian contemplation, Transcendental Meditation, and even specifically nonreligious meditation.[9] Most scientific literature uses the term *meditation* to include all of these disciplines. For the purpose of consistency, I will use *meditation* for what has traditionally been called *contemplation* in Christian ascetic literature. *Meditation* in the traditional Christian sense of discursive, linear thought about a Gospel story, for example, is not included in this use of the term.

---

9. E.g., Herbert Benson, *The Relaxation Response,* William Morrow, New York, 1975; William Johnston, *Silent Music: The Science of Meditation,* Harper & Row, New York, 1974; Morton Trippe Kelsey, *The Other Side of Silence: A Guide to Christian Meditation,* Paulist Press, 1976; Lawrence LeShan, *How to Meditate,* Bantam Books, 1975; Claudio Naranjo, and Robert Ornstein, *On the Psychology of Meditation,* Viking Press, New York, 1971.

Here *meditation* is intended to denote *contemplation*, the "prayer of quiet" that does not employ discursive thought but attempts to empty the mind entirely of all but the presence of God.

One can picture what is going on in the brain by the following metaphor. It must not be taken too literally because this can cause philosophical trouble. But more about this later.

If one pictures a little person (the ego) sitting in front of two television sets, such an image can illustrate what happens in meditation as defined above. Both sets are turned on and both sets are connected together in the center by a complicated set of wires (the corpus callosum).

Waking

The television on the left is tuned to a program that shows someone broadcasting the news and analyzing the situation of the world that is relevant to the viewer watching the program. The program consists of editorials, debates, news broadcasts, and analyses of what has been happening. Occasionally, it even features some quiz shows where nothing but logic is meant to be used in solving various problems. The brightness knob is turned very high and so is the volume knob. It is very difficult not to look at that set. (In terms of brain waves, this would correspond to the production of very rapid beta waves.)

The television on the right is tuned to a program that is a very *avant garde* movie like those produced by Fellini, for example. The brightness knob is turned down to where the images are hardly visible. The volume knob is turned so low that it is very difficult to hear what is being said, particularly when the volume of the other set is turned up so high. It is much easier to ignore this set when the other set is so dominating. (The brain waves that would correspond to this state are alpha waves.)

At regular intervals during the day the volume and brightness of the left set are turned down while the volume and brightness of the right set are turned up somewhat. The ego is able to watch the program on the right set during periods of "daydreaming." Soon, however, the left set is again dominating the attention of the ego.

Sleeping

When night comes, during regular intervals (corresponding to the production of delta waves) the ego watches the left set while it tries to puzzle out various solutions to the problems that have presented themselves during the day. Sometime later, however, the set on the right turns up its volume and brightness so that it cannot be ignored. During these times the ego is enthralled by the esoteric and bizarre drama being played out on the screen. It is so entranced by the plot that nothing moves but its eyes. Its body is otherwise quite still. (This state corresponds to a preponderance of theta wave production.)[10]

Eventually, however, the play normally comes to some kind of a resolution and the ego returns its attention to the left set where specific problems of the day are again being mulled over slowly and carefully to figure out logically the various implications of each situation.

It is important to stress that neither television set is turned off during either the night or the day; they both are playing all the time. The little ego watching the sets is never allowed to sleep! The nature of the state of consciousness at any particular moment is a matter of which set is being observed by the ego and whether the organism as a whole is meant to be awake or asleep.

When the ego is watching the Fellini-like movie, it is absorbed in the strange and bizarre plot. It does not try to analyze the meaning because it is too busy watching the story unfold and identifying with the main character of that story.

If the ego can retain the memory of the plot of the Fellini-like movie long enough when day returns, the brightness and volume of the television set on the left can be turned up higher. Then the news analyst can get to work on translating the visual metaphors of the Fellini-like movie into ordinary prose. The prose version is by definition "prosaic"—it has none of the beauty and poetry of the movie. But it is, in contrast to the movie, much clearer and easier to understand to the prose-speaking ego.

The fact is that there are no channel knobs on either of these television sets. The program on the left TV set only deals with the *analysis* of the situation of the world of the ego. The right set only deals with the

---

10. "One of the researchers likened the sleeper, as he is about to enter a REM period, to a spectator at the theater. Before the curtain rises, he shuffles and fidgets in his seat. As the curtain goes up, he becomes still and attentive. The play begins, and he follows the action with his eyes: he becomes excited as the plot unfolds, his breathing speeds up, and his heart thumps. As long as the play continues, he is wholly immersed in it, unmoving and unspeaking (sleep-walking and -talking normally take place in Stage 2 sleep). When the curtain falls, he moves and stretches, and his former bodily composure is regained . . . the sleeper could indeed be watching a play during his periods of REM sleep, but a play of his own making in which he himself was the director, producer, stage manager, principal actor, and audience all at the same time." Ann Faraday, *Dream Power* (New York: Coward, McCann and Geoghegan, 1972).

synthesis of the situation of the world of the ego. The news broadcaster on the left only speaks in prose. The movie director in charge of the productions on the right only writes plots in the poetry of metaphor. There is some cooperation between the two sets (after all, they are connected to each other in some complicated way), but the sets seem to be designed to do their programs in entirely different modes.

The fact is that most people alternate between sets, not only during the night when they alternate between dreaming sleep and thinking sleep, but also during the day when they alternate between alert, waking thought and relaxed, daydreaming thought. They make a conscious effort to get in touch with the right set when they intend to meditate.

Meditating

Now, meditation, as I am using the term, has been frequently defined *physiologically,* not theologically, as "the art of postponing the onset of sleep." If this is what happens physiologically when one meditates, then the ego watching these two television sets turns the brightness knob down very low by closing the eyes and turns the volume knob down also by attempting to stop the chattering to oneself that goes on continually in the waking state. (This would correspond to the production of alpha waves.) Only when this has happened can full attention be paid to the Fellini-like movie being shown on the television set on the right. (This production is largely being shown in theta waves.) In meditation, the brightness and volume are not necessarily turned up higher in this altered state of consciousness; it is only that the volume and brightness of the set on the left are low enough for attention to be paid to the set on the right.

The Philosophical Difficulties

Karl Popper and John C. Eccles have made a diagram of the brain that may be easier to understand than a realistic drawing of an actual brain.[11]

What they call World 1 is the world as people normally think of it — the outside reality they find around themselves. That world sends information to their brains through the sensory nerves. In turn, they deal with that external World 1 by sending impulses down through their motor nerves. This takes place in both hemispheres, since both hemispheres are required to operate the entire body effectively.

The two hemispheres are labeled Dominant and Minor. They are

---

11. See figure 5.

Figure 5. Diagram of Brain Function

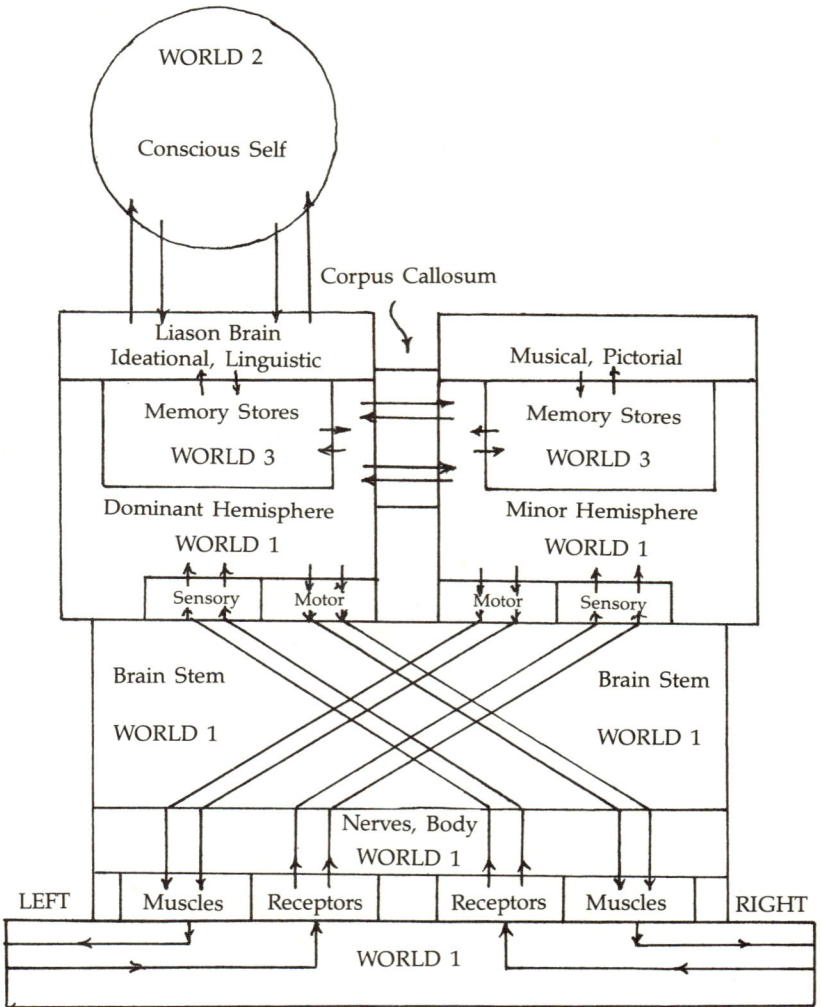

Adapted from Karl R. Popper and John C. Eccles, *The Self and Its Brain* (Berlin: Springer-Verlag, 1981).

also a part of World 1 (physical reality). Within that physical reality are somehow stored memories. These memories can be evoked by external electrical stimulation or by internal decisions. They are labeled World 3 in this diagram.

World 2, however, has no physical counterpart. It seems to take place in the dominant hemisphere, and it is called the Conscious Self. If the Unconscious Self has an equivalent counterpart related to the right hemisphere, the major access that we have to that counterpart is through the corpus callosum. When all connections are severed, all access is prohibited. In normal people there is some access (e.g., through remembering dreams), and in schizophrenic people there is more access than is to be desired (through hallucinations), but in completely commissurotomized patients there seems to be none.[12]

When we discuss the thinking process and its "localization" in specific areas of the brain, we must be very careful not to fall into a reductionist trap. The temptation is to conclude that consciousness is "nothing but" neurophysiological events. As Peacocke has said,

> For if it is true that chemistry is nothing but physics, the bio-chemistry of cells nothing but chemistry, the biology of organisms nothing but the biochemistry of cells, and ecology and sociology nothing but biology, then the branch from this main line—the statement that consciousness is nothing but neuro-physiological events which are nothing but biochemistry, etc., and so down the chain to physics again—becomes the more plausible, and, indeed, attractive to the point of being compelling. I think this possibly accounts for the popularity of the kind of reductionist circle which the view generates in its crudest forms.[13]

---

12. At the beginning of the research with commissurotomized patients, there seemed to be a few who could remember dreams. Later, however, it was discovered through noninvasive procedures that the original operation had not severed the entire corpus callosum, and some contact between the hemispheres was ultimately maintained.

At a still later date, EEGs during sleep indicated that commissurotomized patients could relate dreams when awakened during REM periods, but their dreams "lack the characteristics of dream work; their fantasies are unimaginative, utilitarian, and tied to reality; their symbolization is concretistic, discursive, and rigid." K.D. Hoppe, "Split Brains and Psychoanalysis," *Psychoanalytic Quarterly* 46 (1977): 220–24; also K.D. Hoppe, "Split-brain: Psychoanalytic Findings and Hypotheses," *Journal of the American Academy of Psychoanalysis*, April 1978, 6 (2): 193–213.

13. A.R. Peacocke, "Reductionism: A Review of the Epistemological Issues and Their Relevance to Biology and the Problem of Consciousness," *Zygon: Journal of Religion and Science* 11 (1976): 308.

The operative phrase here is "nothing but." Not only does it denigrate the entire process, but it places it into a circular trap.

Reductionism is not the only pit into which the philosophically unwary may fall. In the illustration concerning the two televisions sets described above, every part of the metaphor corresponds to a physical reality in the brain itself—except for one part: the *homunculus*, the little person watching the two television sets. There is no physical correspondence to the "little person" watching the sets in our brains. "Consciousness," so far, has not been localized to a specific part of the brain, except to assert that it seems to be more associated with the left hemisphere than with the right. There is no anatomical "part" that we can designate as the "organ of consciousness." It is still quite mysterious and is the center of the philosophical "brain-mind problem" of dualism.

This chapter has dealt with the hemispheres of the brain in psychological terms. Such a psychological study has shown that the analogical thinking of the right hemisphere, especially as it appears in dreams, has its own vocabulary that can be roughly translated from poetic metaphor into ordinary prose. People are normally unaware of the contents of the thinking in the right hemispheres; they become aware of that kind of thinking, when, for example, they dream. At least part of the time, prophecy in the Bible was obtained by dreaming, as when Jeremiah dreamed certain prophecies.[14] Such dreams deal in Primary Process thinking, which means that the kind of thinking that is being employed is not everyday, ordinary discourse. It is specialized, analogical thinking frequently employed to solve particular problems and to come to conclusions about particular ambiguous situations. Much, though not all, of the prophetic literature might be described in this way.

Brain waves and other noninvasive procedures help in the study of various altered states of consciousness in both the waking and sleeping states. It might be useful to attempt to classify prophetic visions as REM visions (which can occur either during waking or during sleeping states) or hypnagogic visions (which occur in the twilight zone that lies between waking and sleeping). REM visions and hypnagogic visions have similarities, but they also have real distinctions. Perhaps these distinctions can help lead to a better understanding of the prophetic consciousness.

The emotional intensity of the dreamer must reach a certain level

---

14. Jer. 31:26.

before the dreaming mechanism goes into action to attempt to solve problems or to resolve emotional conflicts. This means that the subjects "under discussion" in dreams are serious subjects to the dreamer and not just casual ponderings. It might be said, as a corollary, that the prophetic visions that appear in the Bible never seem to be concerned with trivial matters. The subject matter "under discussion" in prophetic visions is usually concerned with important national events. However, perhaps that is because the prophet's dreams about trivial subjects were not shared or deemed valuable enough to others to save.

Part Three: Parapsychology and Paraphysics

3. Extrasensory Perception

It is important for me to know whether I "believe" in the paranormal or not. It is not an easy question to answer. There are times, particularly right after some seemingly paranormal event happens to me, when I am convinced that I do. However, when nothing like that happens to me for a long time, I begin to wonder if I have talked myself into believing something that has a much simpler explanation. Nor do the personalities of many psychics help in encouraging me to join the ranks of believers. However, I do consider myself to be a religious person, and the same comment could be made about the personalities of many who are "professionally religious." So an objective study of such phenomena is not possible without dealing with one's own prejudices.

Even when prejudice is not involved, it is exceedingly difficult to prove in any case that one thing *causes* another. *Post hoc, ergo propter hoc* is a classical fault in logic; just because one thing happens *after* another thing does not mean that the first thing *caused* the second thing to happen. If the second event seems to be related to the first event in terms of significance, it might have occurred at that time because of sheer coincidence. However, mathematicians are able to figure out what the odds are that something is coincidental, and when the chances are hundreds, thousands, or millions to one that something is coincidental, it still does not eliminate coincidence.[1] It merely states that it is less and less likely that coincidence is the real explanation.

In fact, it is really beside the point whether I "believe" in paranormal events. I know that there are events I have witnessed that are difficult to explain with ordinary scientific explanations. There are few genuine scientists who would claim that the scientific view of reality has finally reached the ultimate "truth." New paradigms of reality are proposed all the time. Perhaps what we now call *paranormal* will one day be

---

1. John J. Heaney, *The Sacred and the Psychic: Parapsychology and Christian Theology*, (Ramsey, N.J.: Paulist Press, 1984), 11–12.

understood to be part of *normal* reality, and such events will be understood in scientific terms that include laws that are currently unknown.

Nevertheless, I have been conditioned throughout most of my life to reject the possibilities of the paranormal. This is true of a large portion of the population. Most modern, educated people live their lives on the assumption that the only possibilities in reality are logical possibilities. Logical possibilities are possibilities that are in accord with consensus reality. One cannot know what will happen in the future before it happens; therefore it is *not* known.

But there is some evidence that the attitude that people have about possibilities seems to change the possibilities themselves. For example, Gertrude Schmeidler's experiments with children's use of ESP with Zener cards is a case in point.[2] She discovered that those children who thought that they would be able to guess what the cards were, which they were unable to see, scored significantly higher than those who did not believe it was possible. She called this the "sheep and goats effect."[3]

There is, however, a serious danger in discussing the paranormal. There are two extremes that must be avoided in any study of this kind: gullibility, on the one hand, and closed-mindedness, on the other. Neither attitude is very productive to arriving at objective conclusions.

Now, Newton described a physics that explains most of our ordinary reality quite well. But Einstein has showed that certain physical events are not explained by Newton's system. They are explained by Einsteinian physics. Newtonian physics and Einsteinian physics are not compatible with each other. No doubt there will eventually come a unified theory that will encompass the truths of both—but, until then, there are two mutually contradictory sets of rules. The situation is similar to the contrast between normal phenomena and paranormal phenomena.

---

2. Zener cards are the same size as playing cards, but there are only twenty-five cards to a deck. Each card has a different symbol. There is either a cross, a square, a circle, a set of wavy lines, or a plus sign on each. Statistics can be studied as to how accurately a subject can guess the identity of each card without having seen it. Some of these statistics show that some people have remarkable abilities to guess at levels *far* above those expected by chance alone.

3. G.R. Schmeidler, and R.A. McConnell, *ESP and Personality Patterns*, Yale University Press, New Haven, Conn., 1958. See also Barbara E. Lovitts, "The Sheep-Goat Effect Turned Upside Down," *Journal of Parapsychology*, No. 4, December 1981, 293–309; Michael A. Thalbourne, "Extraversion and the Sheep-Goat Variable: A Conceptual Replication," *Journal of the American Society for Psychical Research*, April 1981, Vol. 75, No. 2, 105–20.

Psychology has gone a long way toward helping to understand human behavior. Its presuppositions are those of "consensus reality." No other "realities" exist. Parapsychology, however, is concerned with cognition that is *not* based on the five senses. It also studies claims that physical objects can be made to move without any normal power or energy source. The first phenomenon is called *extrasensory perception*; the second is called *psychokinesis*. The first has to do with psychology; the second has to do with physics.

There is a serious confusion in the minds of some people between parapsychology and the occult. The occult embraces such things as numerology, astrology, palmistry, doctrines about life or reality that entail whole systems of esoteric beliefs. Parapsychology, on the other hand, is an experimental science and has nothing to do with the acceptance of these systems of belief.

Extrasensory perception (ESP) and psychokinesis (PK) seem to be governed by similar laws or behavior principles. Furthermore, those people who seem to exhibit talent in one area tend to show talent in the other area as well. In recent years a considerable amount of research has been conducted to determine if ESP and PK are related to lateralized specialization of brain hemispheres.[4] Further research has been conducted concerning the relationship between altered states of consciousness (such as REM dreaming or the hypnagogic state) to ESP and PK.[5]

It is quite probable that many of the areas of investigation now considered to fall under the category of parapsychological investigation

---

4. E.g., Richard S. Broughton, "Brain Hemisphere Specialization and Its Possible Effects on ESP Performance," in *Research in Parapsychology 1975*, Metuchen, N.J.: Scarecrow Press, 1976, 98–102; Richard S. Broughton, "Possible Brain Hemisphere Laterality Effects in ESP Performance," *Journal of the Society for Psychical Research*, Vol. 48, No. 770, December 1976, 384–99; Michaeleen Maher, and Gertrude R. Schmeidler, "Cerebral Lateralization Effects in ESP Processing," *Journal of the American Society for Psychical Research*, Vol. 71, 1977, 261–71; Jan Ehrenwald, "Right- vs. Left-Hemispheric Approach in Psychical Research," *Journal of the American Society for Psychical Research*, Vol. 78, No. 1, January 1984, 29–40; Jan Ehrenwald, "Psi Phenomena, Hemispheric Dominance and the Existential Shift," *Parapsychology Review*, Vol. 9, No. 5, September-October 1978, 1–3; Michaeleen Maher, "Correlated Hemispheric Asymmetry in the Sensory and ESP Processing of 'Emotional' and 'Nonemotional' Videotapes" (Ph.D. diss., City University of New York, 1983).
5. Adrian Parker, *States of Mind: ESP and Altered States of Consciousness*, Taplinger Publishing, New York, 1975, esp. 82–83 (the hypnagogic state), 84ff. (REM dream state), 146ff. (the meditative state).

will one day be considered to fall under the category of psychological or physical investigation. For example, hypnosis and multiple personality were once considered by the scientific world to be parapsychological topics. Today they are considered to be respectable areas worthy of scientific study and have earned secure places in the study of psychology.

In the past, paranormal phenomena have frequently been associated with the lives of the saints, and, as a consequence, most official investigation of parapsychological phenomena has been carried out by religious bodies. In spite of some of the errors into which many of these investigations have strayed, some of them came very close to agreeing with what modern investigators have concluded. For instance, in the eighteenth century the Roman Catholic Church began to make investigations about what we would call parapsychological phenomena. The investigations were carried out by a man named Lambertini (who later became Pope Benedict XIV). His role was that of "devil's advocate," the person whose duty it was to bring up all evidence contrary to whatever evidence seemed to point to the appropriateness of canonizing the person under investigation into official sainthood.

It was his conclusion that not only saints, but "fools, idiots, melancholy persons, and brute beasts" can have experiences that bring them knowledge of events past, present, and future, things distant in space, and things known only to one person. In other words, extrasensory knowledge is not intrinsically related to sanctity or to an evil life or, for that matter, to sanity or to insanity.

He also concluded that people who have visions of either the dead or the living are not *per se* either holy or demonic. He asserted that prophecy occurred more often in sleep than in the waking state and that prophets cannot always distinguish between their own thoughts and what we would call extrasensory perceptions. Modern parapsychologists have come to identical conclusions. He asserted as well that predictions often come in symbolic forms that must then be interpreted.[6] The correspondences between what he concluded and the conclusions of modern parapsychologists are quite remarkable.

One of the current difficulties of discussing paranormal experience is in deciding in which of several categories one could place such an experience. That is not to say that the category is an entity that

---

6. D. Scott Rogo, *Parapsychology: A Century of Inquiry*, Dell Publishing, New York, 1975, 36.

44

actually exists; it is more accurate to say that it is a *logical* category that may or may not correspond to something in "reality." I have developed a form to help the person who has had such a paranormal experience describe not only the state of consciousness during the experience but also the logical category into which it might fit.[7]

The column on the left is intended to classify the state of consciousness that people are in when they experience what they believe to be a paranormal event. When they are awake, they can be very alert, relaxed and alert, or relaxed and engaged in daydreaming. Paranormal events have been reported in all three states.

If they are consciously in a meditative state, they may be intentionally imagining certain things or they may be experiencing certain images or sounds that seem to come to them without their willing them. This latter state is a more passive one where they are not consciously willing to see or hear anything in their minds, yet they are observing or listening to things that seem to be coming to them spontaneously.

If they are on the way toward going to sleep but are still on the conscious side of that twilight zone, they may see brief film clips like mini-dreams. These are the hypnagogic images.[8] If they have already gone to sleep, they experience longer dreams that have plots and scene changes (Rapid Eye Movement, or REM, dreams). If they experience short scenes when they are beginning to wake up, these are called hypnopompic dreams.

Sometimes, under the influence of drugs, anaesthesia, a hypnotic trance, or other conditions, paranormal events may be experienced.

It is useful to try to classify the paranormal event into logical categories. It is also important not to be too wedded to the categories, since they, as categories, may not ultimately correspond to the reality itself. No one, as yet, knows enough about the events to be sure.

Broadly speaking, paranormal events can be classified into two groups: extrasensory perception (ESP) and psychokinesis (PK). Extrasensory perception is, as the term implies, perceiving something factual without having received data through any of the five senses: touch, taste, smell, hearing, or sight. Psychokinesis has to do with physically altering reality by using the mind rather than by using physical means.

---

7. See figure 6.
8. See John Gertz, "Hypnagogic Fantasy, EEG, and Psi Performance in a Single Subject," *Journal of the American Society for Psychical Research*, April 1983, Vol. 77, No. 2, 155–70.

Figure 6. Form for Recording Paranormal Experience

PARANORMAL EXPERIENCE

NAME_____
      (optional)

(If more than one experience
is to be recorded, use <u>one</u>
sheet for each experience.)

DATE OF EXPERIENCE_____   TIME OF DAY_____

DATE OF THIS RECORDING_____

<u>IN WHAT STATE OF CONSCIOUSNESS
WERE YOU WHEN IT OCCURRED?</u>
(Put a check in the proper
category.)

<u>HOW WOULD YOU DESCRIBE THE
EXPERIENCE?</u>
(Put a check in the proper
category.)

1.   EXTRASENSORY PERCEPTION

WAKING	<u>Active alertness</u>	( )
	<u>Relaxed alertness</u>	( )
	Day-dreaming state	( )
MEDITATIVE	<u>Active</u>, intentional imaging	( )
	<u>Passive</u>, spontaneous imaging	( )
SLEEPING	Hypnagogic (short film clip, near sleep)	( )
	REM dream (movie-like, fully asleep)	( )
	Hypnopompic (short film clip, waking up)	( )
OTHER	<u>Not covered above</u> (Explain: drug-related, hypnotic, etc.	( )

<u>Telepathy</u> (thought trans-   ( )
ference between minds)
<u>Clairvoyance</u> (extrasensory ( )
knowledge of objects or
events without the help
of another person)
<u>Precognition</u> (knowledge of ( )
a future event without
sensory information)
<u>Retrocognition</u> (knowledge ( )
of a past event without
sensory information)
<u>Mediumship</u> (source appears ( )
to be discarnate)
<u>Out-of-Body Experience</u>   ( )
(consciousness separat-
ing from body, remote
viewing)

2.   PSYCHOKINESIS
<u>Telekinesis</u> (direct action ( )
of mind moving matter)
<u>RSPK</u> (disturbances confin- ( )
ed to a locality)
<u>Paranormal healing</u>   ( )

On the reverse side of this page please type in as much detail as
possible, a careful description of the experience. Use single
spacing in order to keep the description to one page, if possible.

46

Both ESP and PK are called by the Greek letter *psi*, which stands for paranormal phenomena in general.

In the first instance, that of extrasensory perception, several categories logically fall into this group. Each category implies, by its very name, a presupposition about how the information is transmitted. There is no real problem about using these categories as long as we are aware that those presuppositions may be wrong. But they are useful when they describe what might be the "mechanism" at work.

Most of my own life can be easily understood in terms of the normal. Indeed, "coincidence" might explain *everything* in my life, including some unusual occurrences. Coincidence, however, is not a very convincing explanation for some events. There are a number of instances that might be more satisfactorily explained in terms of the paranormal. In the following section I will try to define the categories and, where possible, give personal experiences that might be placed in those categories.

Telepathy

The first category under extrasensory perception is that of telepathy. These events *seem* to involve thought transference between two or more minds.

An Experiment in Telepathic Drawing

For example, some years ago my wife and I decided to conduct an experiment. We both got tablets of white paper, and each had a pencil. We agreed that she was to draw something on the page, and I, sitting across the room with my eyes closed, would try to visualize what it was she was drawing and to draw it myself after opening my eyes. This was not a "scientific" experiment in that it had no special controls and no outside observers. We only did it in the spirit of a game to find out what would happen.

We had about eight different attempts. While most of these attempts had no exact replication, several had some interesting similarities.

Her first drawing was a conscious attempt to duplicate the shield of the Episcopal Church. I drew a circle with an X in the center. They were not identical, but were somewhat similar (see figure 7).

Figure 7. Shield and Crossed Circle

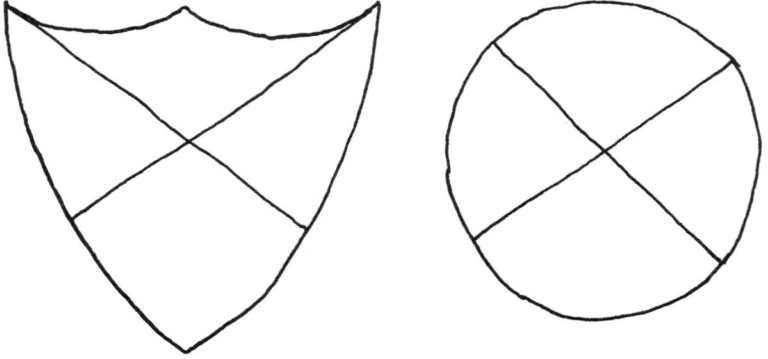

Then she drew a tree. I drew a leaf with something like rays coming out of the top. Again it was not a "direct hit" but was similar (see figure 8.)

Figure 8. Tree and Leaves

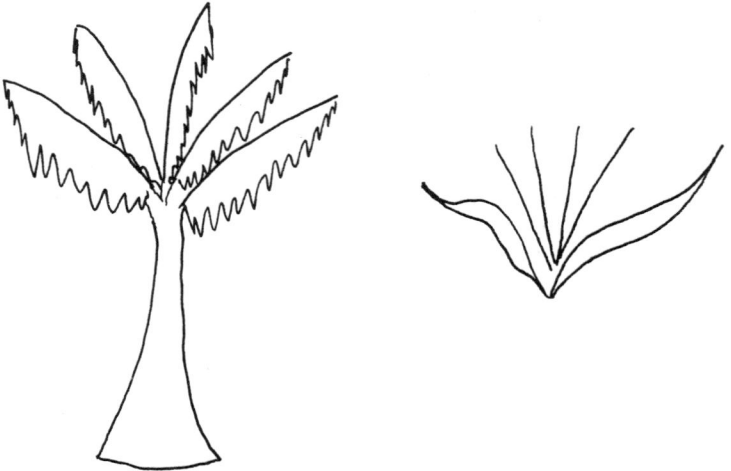

Next she drew the number three. I also drew the number three and put a mirror image of the number three on the left. It looked like a cat, so I added ears and a tail to make it unmistakable. (Notice how I concluded what it "must have been" and then added details to make it correspond more closely to the reality I thought it was (see figure 9).

Figure 9. Three and Cat

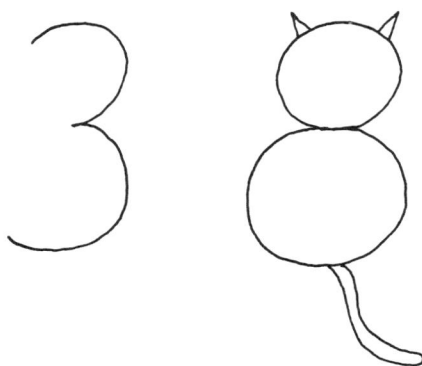

Then she drew an ice cream cone. I drew what looked to me like a sailboat, but the sails were not unfurled. Again, similar in shape but not identical. One was almost an upside down image of the other (see figure 10).

Figure 10. Ice Cream Cone and Sailboat

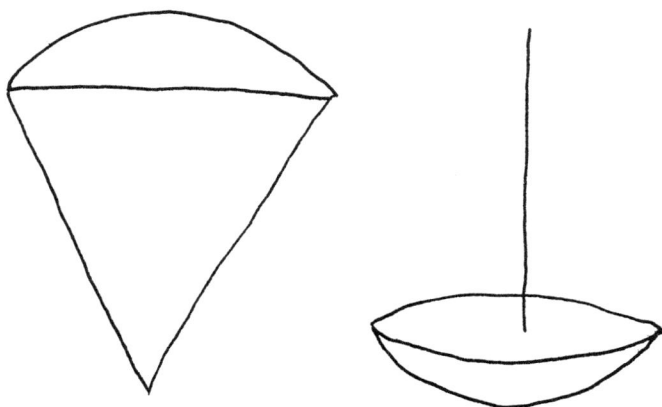

Next she drew a heart. I drew something that could only be called a "blob," but it had the potential of being a heart with only a little rearrangement (see figure 11).

Figure 11. Heart and "Blob"

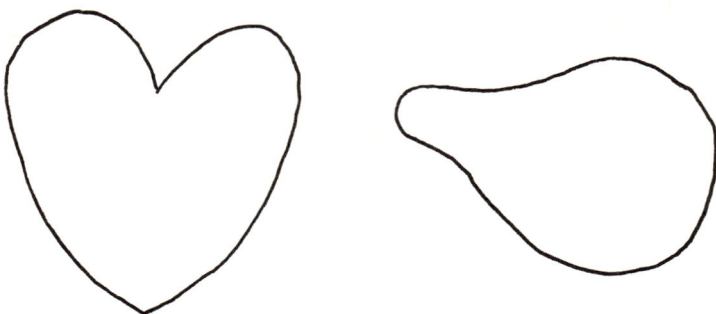

One of the most interesting total *visual* misses was a direct hit in *double entendre*. She drew a "club" of the playing card variety. I drew a "club" of the baseball bat variety (see figure 12).

Figure 12. Club and Club

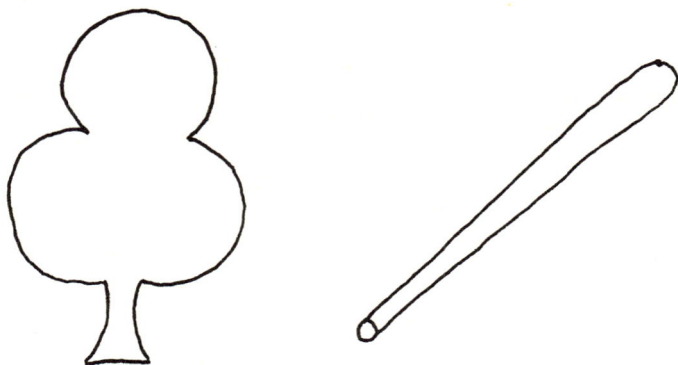

Then she drew a grid that seemed flat. I drew a flat surface seen in perspective (see figure 13).

Figure 13. Grid and Flat Surface

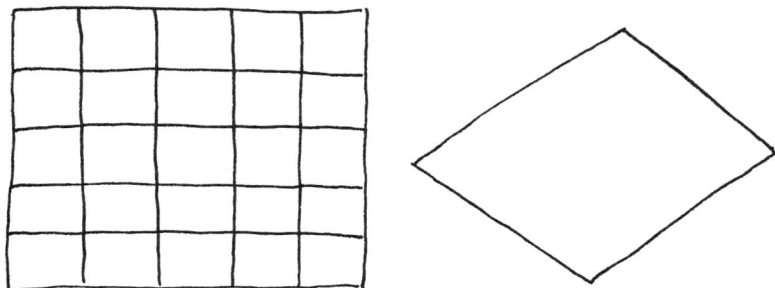

Then she drew an oblong leaf. I drew an oblong dirigible (see figure 14).

Figure 14. Leaf and Dirigible

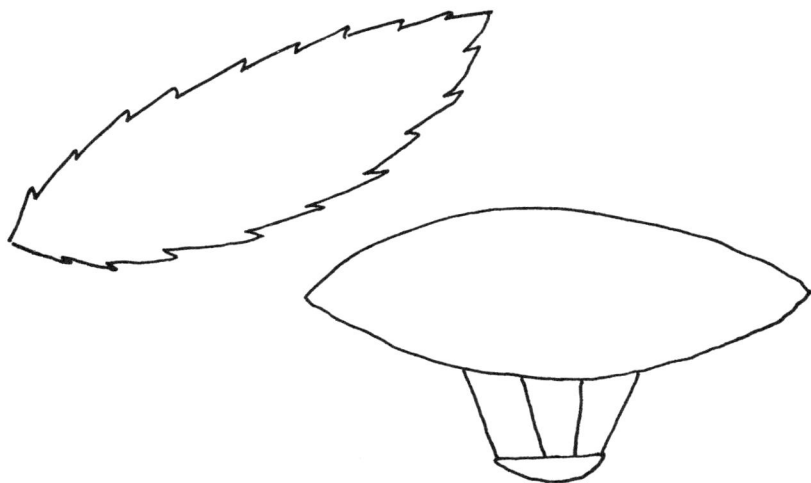

Now, none of these examples is a "direct hit," but they were provocative, nonetheless. There are several factors that might have influenced my drawings. Theoretically, I could have heard her pencil making the drawings on the paper, and that might have given me a clue as to what she was drawing. But I was not conscious of doing that. A more scientific experiment would have had her sit in another room and would have had observers keeping watch over the entire experiment. Nevertheless, it was an interesting and provocative game that made us think that there might be "something to" extrasensory perception.[9]

The psychoanalyst Dr. Jan Ehrenwald has studied this type of telepathic drawing experiment, and while he sees "direct hits" as very interesting, he believes that the most revealing drawings are the ones that are "near misses." He has proposed a theory, which states that

> on comparing telepathic drawings with drawings made by brain-injured patients suffering from optical agnosia, the identical tendency to distortion and disorganization of the target materials can be discerned. It suggests that the telepathic subject is "agnostic" in relation to psi impressions, and that his central processing takes place in the right rather than the left hemisphere.[10]

In other words, the "receivers" distort the information being sent by the "transmitters" because they are unaware of the *meaning* of the information being transmitted. They get elements of the information but do not know the meaning of these elements and, as a consequence, use them wrongly in trying to form a whole.

It is as if a person with damage in the left hemisphere is shown a

---

9. Somewhat similar experiments were conducted over a long period of time between Mr. and Mrs. Upton Sinclair with very impressive results. See Upton Sinclair, *Mental Radio*, Charles C. Thomas, Springfield, Ill., 1962, especially the chapter written by Mrs. Sinclair in which she describes how to achieve the mental state appropriate for such experiments (pp. 116–28).
10. Jan Ehrenwald, "Cerebral Localization and the Psi Syndrome" in *Journal of Nervous and Mental Disease,* Vol. 161, No. 6, Williams & Wilkins, 1975, 393. "The philosopher Henri Bergson . . . proposed that the brain cortex serves as a screen to ward off biologically irrelevant or undesirable external stimuli from conscious awareness—among them telepathy and clairvoyance . . . Psi responses [of the order of card-calling tests] are essentially flaw determined; they are due to flaws in the operation of the subject's perceptual defenses, the screening function of the Bergsonian filter or of what Freud described as the *Reizschutz* protecting the ego from being flooded by stimuli from the id. They can be contrasted with the essentially need-determined psi responses of the spontaneous type, as can be studied in the psychoanalytic situation" (p. 397).

line drawing of a pair of glasses and asked what it represents. He says to himself, "It has two circles that are connected and two things that are bent in a curve. It must be a bicycle!" All of the elements are there, but the specific identification (a left hemisphere task) is wrong.[11] It is possible that if the "receiver" in such a telepathic experiment were able to "turn off" the left hemisphere and stop trying to *understand* what was being received, the information would not be distorted by the attempt to turn it into what it was "obviously" supposed to be.[12] For example, when the number three was being drawn by my wife, I received that image but misinterpreted it to be half of the image of a cat. Since it was a cat, I went ahead and drew a tail and ears to make it explicit. Perhaps, if my left hemisphere had not insisted that it knew what the figure was supposed to be, the right hemisphere would have been satisfied to record the information as it was sent without further elaboration.

The drawing experiment was a conscious attempt to try to communicate telepathically. Some time later, however, there was an event that seemed to be telepathic but was not set up consciously at all.

A Telepathic Dream?

Some time ago I was asked to speak at a conference in Paris. When I came home, I was suffering from jet lag and was unable to sleep late. I woke up about 6:30 A.M., got out of bed, ate breakfast, and began to read a magazine I had been given at the conference I attended in Paris. The magazine was about parapsychology in France.[13] There was a popular article in it entitled *"Je Parle aux Chevaux . . . Ils Me Répondent!"* ("I talk to horses . . . they answer me!").[14] It was a story about a man who claimed to be able to communicate with horses

---

11. A.R. Luria, *The Working Brain*, Basic Books, New York, 1973, 116.
12. For research on hemispheric specialization and extrasensory perception, see Richard S. Broughton, "Brain Hemisphere Specialization and Its Possible Effects on ESP Performance," in *Research in Parapsychology 1975*, (Metuchen, N.J.: Scarecrow Press, 1976): 98–102; and Richard S. Broughton, "Possible Brain Hemisphere Laterality Effects in ESP Performance," *Journal of the Society for Psychical Research*, Vol. 48, No. 770, 384–99. See also, Diana Robinson, "ESP Scoring Patterns in Left-handed Subjects," *Parapsychology Review*, 8 (1), January-February 1977, 16–18.
13. *Psi, La Grande Revue Internationale du Surnaturel Face à la Science*, 151, Bimestriel Septembre-Octobre 1977, Boulevard Haussmann, 75008, Paris, France.
14. Ibid., by Joel Andre, 90–100.

without actually speaking to them. He claimed to be able to ride a horse, and it would go wherever he wanted it to go without his touching the reins, because he could tell it mentally and it would respond. There were also photographs of some of the horses, and one picture showed a horse with a peculiar kind of profile.

My wife was still asleep, and I was wanting to tell her about this article. But rather than wake her up before she woke up by herself, I mentally said to her, "Get up! Wake up!" But she slept on.

Then I got a book out of the bookshelf that my daughter had given me for Christmas called *Old New York in Early Photographs.* I looked through the pictures slowly. I saw Central Park in the nineteenth century with horse-drawn carriages and people in old-fashioned dress. The pictures were quite grey with barren, leafless trees and misty-looking landscapes. There were pictures of the old city hall, old shipping warehouses, etc.

My wife was still asleep, and I was lonely, so again I said mentally, "Get up!"—but to no avail. In fact, she slept on for another ten minutes or so and then woke up and came into the kitchen for breakfast. She said, "I had the funniest dream," and then began to tell me about it. After she had told me a sentence or two, I stopped her and asked her to write it down before telling me the rest of it.

There were a number of quite surprising correspondences between what I was seeing at the time she was dreaming and what she was actually dreaming:

1. The article I was reading was written in French. In the dream there were street signs written in French.

2. The article was about a man who claimed to be able to speak to horses, and they would respond to his command. In the dream my wife spoke to horses, and they were able to speak to her.

3. Many of the pictures I looked at in the book about old New York were of Central Park. The setting of the dream was in Central Park.

4. There were many horse-drawn carriages in the pictures of the book. The dream had as an essential "prop" a horse-drawn carriage.

5. The old pictures of Central Park were not in color, and the predominating tone was quite grey. The dream was described as having taken place in a grey setting.

6. There were bare tree branches in the pictures of the park. The dream also had bare tree branches that were mentioned specifically and were described as looking almost like "antlers."

7. A city hall was in the picture book. A city hall appeared in the dream.

When I showed my wife the article in French I had been reading, she recognized in one of the pictures the "funny" profile of the horse in her dream.[15] She also said that the trees in the old photographs in the book about New York were like what she had described as "antlers" in her dream. She had not seen the magazine previously.

The plot of the dream was the dreamer's own creation, serving its own purpose, but it is as if I were supplying some of the props for this little play by "transmitting" the images and ideas I encountered in my reading while she was creating the dream. In many ways, the props resemble the bits and pieces of images that Freud called *day residue*— elements of the dream that remind the dreamer of things seen in the previous day or previous days that were incorporated into the dream itself. However, in this case, the day residue seems to have been transmitted from elsewhere while the dream was being composed by the dreamer.[16]

It is also worth noting that when I intentionally tried to send her a message to wake up, nothing happened. The "transmitting" seems to have taken place when I was *in no way* intending to "transmit."[17]

Obviously, there were other elements in the dream that did not correspond to what I had been thinking about while she was dreaming, but the number of actual correspondences seemed to be quite remarkable. So telepathy seems to be a category that might have some subjective validity for me.

Clairvoyance

Personally, I have never had an experience that might be classified as clairvoyant. Clairvoyance is defined as the reception of information about an event that seems to have no living "transmitter" to send information about that event.

However, there have been many parapsychological experiments that deal with clairvoyance, especially as it relates to the operation of brain

15. Ibid., 90.
16. For more scientifically controlled experiments on dream telepathy, see M. Ullman; S. Krippner; and A. Vaughan, *Dream Telepathy*, Macmillan, New York, 1973.
17. For further information on work done on ESP and dreaming, see Parker, *States of Mind: ESP and Altered States of Consciousness*, 82ff.

hemispheres. One such experiment dealt with testing subjects to see if they could distinguish between four musical selections being played on a tape recorder in a distant room. The subjects were instructed to relax in a comfortable reclining chair with eyes closed while an assistant put one of the following randomly selected tapes into the recorder: Barber's "Adagio for Strings," a bagpipe rendition of "Hieland Laddie," Gershwin's "Rhapsody in Blue," and a rock instrumental, "Do What You Like," featuring a drum solo. In sessions studying telepathy, the assistant listened to the tape as it was played; in sessions studying clairvoyance, the assistant neither listened to the tape nor knew its contents. While the tapes were being played, the subjects listened to "soft white noise" through earphones.

The results showed no difference between the telepathic and the clairvoyant modes. There were twenty hits and ten misses. "Several subjects reported actually hearing music in the white noise. One subject mentioned bagpipe music while the agent listened to the bagpipe rendition of 'Hieland Laddie.' "[18]

Actually, no one knows if there is a distinction between clairvoyance and telepathy. They are both contemporary happenings; it is not certain whether a "transmitter" is necessary for the "receiver" to receive. Certainly, there seems to be no sender necessary for clairvoyance. Perhaps a sender is not even necessary for telepathy. The two may be the same thing.

If clairvoyance and telepathy are concerned with events contemporaneous with the reception of that information, precognition and retrocognition are concerned with events that happened after or before the reception.

Precognition

Precognition can be defined as the correct knowledge of a future event without the input of sensory information before that event takes place. I have personally had more experiences that might be classified as precognitive than any other category of the paranormal.

Three Knights Speaking Poetry

For example, once I had a doctor's appointment and went to the office

---

18. Kathleen Altom, and William G. Braud, "Clairvoyant and Telepathic Impressions of Musical Targets," in *Research in Parapsychology 1975, Research Briefs (III)*, ed. Joanna Morris; W.G. Roll; and R.L. Morris, (Metuchen, N.J.: Scarecrow Press 1976), 171–74.

about twenty minutes early. The following is taken from a journal I was keeping at the time:

> I was extremely tired, and as I sat in the waiting room, I fell into a deep meditative state in a matter of several minutes. Immediately, spontaneous images came to me. Medieval knights were fighting in costume with swords and speaking the most beautiful poetry I had ever heard. I do not know what they were saying, but the poetry had meter and rhyme and cadence. It was exquisite!

Without my knowing it, my wife had been given tickets for both of us to see *Henry V* at the Brooklyn Academy of Music, which was being presented ten days after this happened. Meanwhile, I had told my wife of this extraordinarily beautiful experience in the doctor's waiting room. When we went to see the play, we both became aware *simultaneously* that the scene we were watching was identical to what I had described seeing in that waiting room. The same cadenced poetry and the same costumed knights doing sword play were right in front of us. It was an astounding experience. However, it is not the kind of thing that is readily provable. There is only the word of one person, myself, that the scenes were identical.

The Rubber Mask

However, the day after having that experience in the doctor's waiting room, another event occurred. The following is from my journal:

> At night I dreamed that I painted my face with liquid rubber latex several times, letting it dry each time. Then I pulled the mask off (as in the television series "Mission Impossible") and found that I liked it better with the mask off.

The psychological meaning of the dream was immediately evident to me. I had been undergoing a sort of professional identity crisis. I had been a professor for some time and had always preferred being called "doctor" or "professor" up to that point. However, I had begun to feel that this practice somehow distanced me from those with whom I wanted to communicate. I had begun to encourage people to speak to me as a human being, not a representative of an institution or of a professional field. In the dream I am saying that it feels a lot better relying on my real face rather than a professional mask.

But the psychological interpretation of the dream is not really the point of the discussion here. The remarkable thing is that the morning *after* having had the dream, I read in *The New York Times* about a scientist who had taken Dr. Howard Leakey's fossils of the skull of a human being three million years old and painted the inside of the skull several times with liquid latex rubber. When the rubber had dried, he removed it and filled the mold with plaster, thus making a cast of the shape of the brain. He claimed that there were indications of hemispherical dominance and of a Broca's (speech) area as long ago as three million years!

As astounding as his conclusions were, what astounded me most is that it appeared to me that, rather than using day residue of the previous day to construct my dream, I had actually used day residue of the *following* day to do so! Could it be that some dreams use images from the future to act as props for their stories, or was this sheer coincidence?

Memories

About four months after this dream I had another dream, about my cousin, whose childhood nickname was "Yibbie." The following is from my journal:

> Yibbie came to visit me with her husband. She had her head bowed and her eyes closed for a minute. She was sending a message to somebody else. I said, "You know, I've been having some ESP experiences, and I've never done that before! That is something that is brand new to me." She looked very doubtful, and then I said, "Have I?" and she said, "Yes." I said, "Well, I can't remember them. Tell me." She said, "Well, I don't know why you can't remember them. We've got memory books." Her husband was lying on the bed listening to the conversation.

The next day there arrived in the mail a cardboard box full of keepsakes and mementos my father had unexpectedly mailed to me. In it were several pictures of Yibbie (whom I had not seen or thought of in years) and also a book, furnished by the funeral home when my grandmother died, entitled *Memories.*

Despite the fact that this can all be explained by coincidence, it is unusual that, not having seen my cousin for at least twenty years, and not having thought of her in many years, her picture turns up in the mail the following day, along with a book entitled *Memories.*

The Faucet

In April of the following year, on a Sunday evening at 8:10 P.M., I was lying on the couch watching a television show with my daughter. The following is from my journal:

I began to doze off, and while still hearing the conversation on the television set, I began to see a faucet with something like a plastic hose attached to the nozzle. It was very fat and had a bulge on it. A little lower down it branched out in a number of directions. I couldn't see above the faucet or below where the branching out began. It was an image I had never seen before, and I thought it was quite unusual. It looked something like this (see figure 15).

Figure 15. Branched Hose

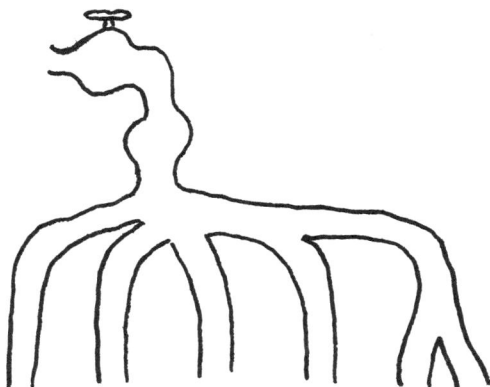

The next day I got on a crosstown bus and sat down and opened my *New York Magazine*, which I had just picked up from my mailbox to thumb through.[19] I turned to page 39 and saw a similar arrangement of branches on a plastic-looking hose. Figure 16 shows a copy of that picture.

19. *New York Magazine*, April 11, 1977. Illustration by Paul Richer.

Figure 16. Branched Pipes

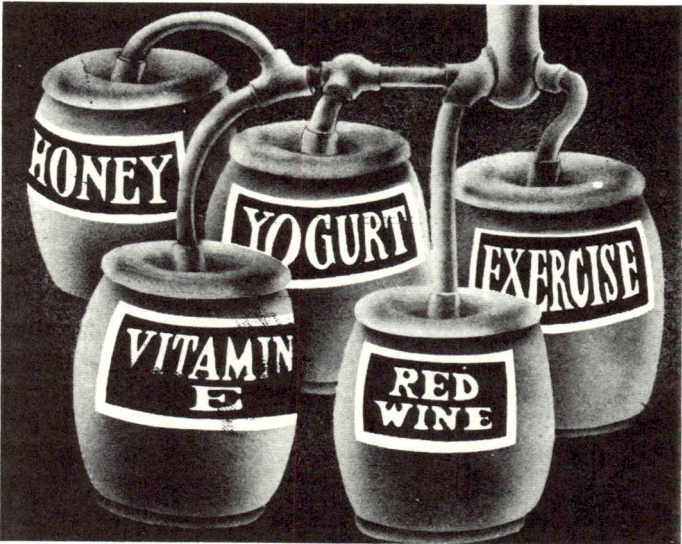

Illustration by Paul Richer, *New York Magazine*, April 11, 1977. Reproduced with permission.

Two aspects of the picture disagree with the image. The picture of the faucet with branches going off in several directions is more like a mirror image of the drawing than an exact replication.[20] Furthermore, the barrels do not appear in the image. But the branched hoses are very similar.

An Embarrassed Smile

Another event happened right around the time of the above. The occurrence took place around 12:30 P.M. My journal says the following:

> While meditating I saw a hypnagogic image of a nineteen or twenty year old Latin American boy smiling in an embarrassed fashion, turning his head down and to the left.

At 5:00 P.M. of that same day, I was walking home on Twenty-first Street in Manhattan, when from a distance of about fifteen to twenty yards I saw a boy and recognized without any hesitation that it was

---

20. Such reversal of image is fairly common in reports of ESP experiences.

the same person I had seen in the hypnagogic image. I had never seen this boy before in my life. I knew immediately that something would happen that would create what I had seen happen in the hypnagogic image.

As I kept walking up toward him, his sister, who was sitting with him on the steps of the building, said to me, "What time is it, mister?" I said to her, "It's five o'clock." The boy said to her in typical older brother fashion, "It's time you got a watch"—*and then smiled in an embarrassed fashion as he turned and lowered his head to the left.*

Now, the most obvious thing about all the seemingly precognitive events described above is that they are unusual, they are interesting (at least to me), but they are absolutely *worthless* and *trivial* in terms of importance. They do not warn me of impending disasters; they do not tell me things I need to know in order to prepare for the future; they do not even give me helpful information. It is as if they were random bits of future information that have seeped into my head. And that corresponds precisely to the theory proposed by Dr. Jan Ehrenwald.[21]

Ehrenwald suggests that "the brain cortex serves as a screen to ward off biologically irrelevant or undesirable external stimuli from conscious awareness—among them telepathy and clairvoyance." He also proposes that the screen is not 100 percent foolproof and that extrasensory events are *flaw-determined*—"they are due to flaws in the operation of the subject's perceptual defenses, the screening function of the Bergsonian filter or of what Freud described as the *Reizschutz* protecting the ego from being flooded by stimuli from the id."[22]

Ehrenwald's second category is *need-determined*—information that is vitally important to the recipient. His explanation for this phenomenon is that, while the personality operates in a mode that is usually tightly closed to psi, people are sometimes capable of shifting their mode of existence to a different level of adaptation. He calls this the *existential shift.*

It is a shift in which we relinquish our customary defensive position towards psi phenomena, while at the same time paying less

---

21. Jan Ehrenwald, "Cerebral Localization and the Psi Syndrome," *Journal of Nervous and Mental Disease*, Vol. 161, No. 6, 1975, 397; Jan Ehrenwald, "Psi Phenomena, Hemispheric Dominance and the Existential Shift," *Parapsychology Review*, Vol. 9, No. 5, September-October 1978, 1–3.
22. Ehrenwald, "Psi Phenomena, Hemispheric Dominance and the Existential Shift," 2.

attention to our time- and space-bound Newtonian, Darwinian or Freudian universe. . . . It is a shift that is apt to recapture, if only for fleeting moments, man's original symbiotic closeness with parents, parent surrogates, or sibling figures, with things animate and inanimate and ultimately with the universe at large.[23]

At these times the reception of psi information is based on need rather than some flaw in the "screen" that shields off such information.

Retrocognition

Retrocognition may be defined as accurate knowledge of a past event without sensory information. This is an experience of which I have no first-hand knowledge, and it is reported much less frequently than other categories of paranormal occurrences. It has characteristics similar to clairvoyance, but in contrast to clairvoyance, the reception of the information about an event does not occur simultaneously with the event but only *after* the event has already occurred. There do not seem to be any clear-cut examples of retrocognition in the Bible.

Mediumship

Mediumship may be defined as the experience of receiving extrasensory knowledge from a source interpreted *by the receiver* to be "discarnate," the spirit of someone deceased. I have no personal experience of such things, but there are many seemingly well-documented sources describing those who claim to have had such experiences.

It is extremely important to make a clear distinction between receiving knowledge in what appears to be an extrasensory manner from a medium without being compelled to accept that person's own explanation as to *how* the extrasensory information was obtained. In other words, there are many other viable explanations of how such knowledge might be obtained other than that it came from the spirit of someone deceased. If it appears to be genuinely extrasensory, it might have just as easily come from telepathy or from clairvoyance.

When Richard Broughton was doing research concerning the possibility that paranormal perceptions might be connected to the workings of the right hemisphere of the brain, he came across some evidence that had appeared in the nineteenth century that was quite provocative.

. . . Some of the investigators of the famous medium, Eusapia Palladino, noted that in her trances the normally right handed

---

23. Ibid.

medium became left handed. This was interpreted to signify increased participation of the right lobe in mediumistic states. Finally . . . the great Frederic W.H. Myers [reported] on his extensive studies of graphic automatism. In a detailed and closely reasoned paper he discussed the different types of productions coming from the "planchette," a device something like a writing ouija board. He believes that the cases with which he deals represent something paranormal, but telepathy rather than any supposed spirit communication. The utterances scrawled out by the planchette resemble very closely the efforts to communicate made by people who have suffered injury to the language hemisphere of the brain. [They both produce badly spelled messages with poor syntax and limited vocabulary.] He proposes that, if it is the case that in agraphic and aphasic patients it is the right hemisphere which is making the attempt to communicate, then perhaps it is the right hemisphere which is controlling the output of the planchette operators.[24]

It is important to make a clear distinction between the psychological factors that may be operating in mediumship and the seemingly genuine extrasensory information that is sometimes obtained in this manner. The medium is convinced that another "being" has taken possession of consciousness and speaks in the place of the medium.[25] This particular aspect of mediumship might rather be understood in terms of multiple personality, a phenomenon that has recently been thoroughly documented and studied by psychologists and psychoanalysts.[26]

But while multiple personality may go a long way toward explaining the psychological "mechanics" of mediumship, it does not offer any adequate explanation as to how accurate extrasensory information is sometimes obtained through mediumship. Could telepathy or clair-

24. Richard S. Broughton, "Psi and the Two Halves of the Brain," *Journal of the Society for Psychical Research*, Vol. 48, No. 765, September 1975, 140–41.
25. For a discussion of whether "possession" is actually a part of Israelite prophecy, see Simon B. Parker, "Possession Trance and Prophecy in Pre-Exilic Israel," *Vetus Testamentum* 28 (1978): 271–85.
26. The phenomenon has been popularized in such works as C.H. Thigpen, and H.M. Cleckley, *The Three Faces of Eve*, Secker and Warburg, London, 1957; and Flora Rheta Schreiber, *Sybil*, Warner Books, 1973. See also P. Horton, and D. Miller, "The Etiology of Multiple Personality," *Comprehensive Psychiatry*, 1972, 13: 151–9.

voyance be involved? Perhaps the right hemisphere plays an important role in all paranormal perception.[27]

Out-of-Body Experiences

There are several other terms used to describe this particular experience: *astral projection* (an occult term), *autoscopy* (a medical term), *exteriorization* or *disassociation* (psychological terms), *traveling clairvoyance* or *out-of-body experience* (parapsychological terms), and *remote viewing* (a term recently coined by physicists).[28]

The experience is called "out-of-body" (OBE) because many, though not all, of the subjects experience a feeling of their consciousness literally leaving their bodies and traveling elsewhere. There are frequent accounts in these cases of people reporting that their consciousness leaves their bodies and floats above their bodies in the room so that they can look

---

27. Maher, "Correlated Hemisphere Asymmetry."
28. H.E. Puthoff, and R. Targ, "A Perceptual Channel for Information Transfer over Kilometer Distances: Historical Perspective and Recent Research," *Proceedings of the Institute of Electrical and Electronics Engineers, Inc.*, 1976, 329–54. These two physicists on the West Coast have been working for over fourteen years at the Stanford Research Institute on "remote viewing." They have said that "one hypothesis is that information transfer under conditions of sensory shielding is mediated by extremely low-frequency (ELF) electromagnetic waves, a proposal that does not seem to be ruled out by any obvious physical or biological facts" (p. 330). They carried out more than fifty experiments where one person was put in a Faraday cage, which shielded that person from the reception of all electromagnetic waves (except extremely low frequency waves). The subject sat in the cage while the "out-bound" person viewed the surroundings at a large distance at a prearranged time. The subject was told to describe what appeared to his or her mind. The correspondences were quite remarkable. See also Russell Targ, and Robert L. Morris, "Note on a Reanalysis of the UCSB Remote-Viewing Experiments," *Journal of Parapsychology*, Vol. 46, March 1982, 47–50. For an excellent review see Carlos S. Alvarado, "ESP During Out-of-Body Experiences: A Review of Experimental Studies," *Journal of Parapsychology*, Vol. 46, September 1982, 209–30; Roy D. Salley, "REM Sleep Phenomena During Out-of-Body Experiences," *Journal of the American Society for Psychical Research*, April 1982, Vol. 76, No. 2, 157–66; Carlos S. Alvarado, "Phenomenological Aspects of Out-of-Body Experiences: A Report of Three Studies," *Journal of the American Society for Psychical Research*, July 1984, Vol. 78, No. 3, 219–44; Susan J. Blackmore, "Out-of-Body Experiences, Lucid Dreams, and Imagery: Two Surveys," *Journal of the American Society for Psychical Research*, October 1982, Vol. 76, No. 4, 301–18.

down and see their bodies lying on the bed.[29] Out-of-body experiences are frequently recounted by people who have been clinically "dead" but who are revived by a medical team.[30]

The reason that out-of-body experiences are placed in a list of the categories of extrasensory perception is not because it is an unusual phenomenon but because sometimes people who undergo this experience obtain information they could not have known if they had been required to rely upon their senses in the location where they originally were. The first impression is that they would have had to "leave their bodies" in order to obtain such information.

The Mount Sinai Trip

The only experience that I have had that falls into this category might also be classified as telepathic. Once I was conducting a study tour to Israel and was on a trip to St. Katherine's monastery at the foot of Mount Sinai. My journal states the following:

> We were supposed to get up in the very early hours of the next morning to climb the mountain and watch the sunrise from the top. Consequently, most of us went to bed quite early in the dormitory. The monastery shuts off its electric generator at an early hour, so there wasn't much incentive to stay up late. Most people went to bed early.
>
> However, I was unable to sleep. After trying to sleep for a long time, I decided to meditate instead. Since it was near the end of

29. Anne M. Cook, and Harvey J. Irwin, "Visuospatial Skills and the Out-of-Body Experience," *Journal of Parapsychology*, Vol. 47, March 1983, 23–35. See also Susan J. Blackmore, "A Psychological Theory of the Out-of-Body Experience," *Journal of Parapsychology*, Vol. 48, No. 3, September 1984, 201–18.

30. Raymond A. Moody, Jr., *Life After Life*, Bantam Book, 1975, and *Reflections on Life After Life*, Bantam Book, 1977; Karlis Osis, *At the Hour of Death*, Avon Books, 1977. For discussions of out-of-body experiences that do not involve near-death incidents, see Robert A. Monroe, *Journeys Out of the Body*, Anchor Press/Doubleday, 1971; Ingo Swann, *To Kiss Earth Goodbye*, Hawthorn Books, New York, 1975; D. Scott Rogo, "Psychological Models of the Out-of-Body Experience: A Review and Critical Evaluation," *Journal of Parapsychology*, Vol. 46, March 1982, 29–45; Thomas P. Locke, Franklin C. Shontz, "Personality Correlates of the Near-Death Experience: A Preliminary Study," *Journal of the American Society for Psychical Research*, October 1983, Vol. 77, No. 4, 311–18; Michael Gross, "Toward an Explanation of Near-Death Phenomena," *Journal of the American Society for Psychical Research*, January 1981, Vol. 75, No. 1, 37–60.

the month-long study-tour, I was quite ready to go home and, frankly, a little homesick. While meditating I decided to go home mentally. I allowed my imagination to picture my consciousness leaving the Sinai Peninsula and flying over the Mediterranean and the Atlantic to arrive in New York. I took my time picturing this journey. When I got to Manhattan I flew over the Seminary, went into my apartment building, took the elevator to my floor, put a key into the front door, and carefully went into every room of my apartment. It was reassuring that everything looked in order, so I reversed the process and came back to Mount Sinai.

The entire process began around 9:30 p.m. and lasted until around 11:00 or 12:00 p.m. I am not sure how long it lasted because I must have dozed off toward the end. The unusual thing was that when I awoke, I was in the complete darkness of the monastery, but could not remember where I was. I didn't know who these people were around me. I could see the luminous dial on the watch of someone who got up to leave the room, but had no idea who he was or what he was doing there. But the most frightening thing was that when I asked myself what *I* was doing there, I realized that I didn't know who *I* was! I had a complete amnesia about myself which lasted for about five minutes. Gradually my memory came back and everything returned to normal.

When I came home after three days, one of the first things my wife said to me was that she had undergone a peculiar experience while I was gone. She said that she had come home from work at 5:30 P.M., New York time, on the day that I had been at Mount Sinai. When she opened the front door, she felt very strongly that I had come back from the trip to Israel three days early! She went through all the rooms of the house to see where I was but couldn't find me in any of them.

When we figured out the time change between Egypt and New York, she had come home from work exactly during the time that I had been meditating at Mount Sinai.

Up until this time, I had always thought that people who spoke of experiences such as this were somehow weird and peculiar. After having had an existential exposure to the experience, I began to look at the phenomenon a little more seriously.

All of the categories of ESP discussed in this chapter have some bearing on a study of prophetic consciousness. This is not to say that all prophetic activities can be classified as telepathic, clairvoyant, retrocognitive, precognitive, mediumistic, or out-of-body experiences. But it does seem appropriate that any thorough study of prophetic con-sciousness ought to take these categories into account.

The second category of paranormal phenomena, psychokinesis, may also be of help in the attempt to understand biblical literature better.

4. Psychokinesis

Psychokinesis may be defined as the causing of physical objects to move or be changed by mental action that involves no physical force upon the object. There are three categories of psychokinetic activity.

Telekinesis

Telekinesis may be defined as the causing of *inanimate* physical objects to move or be changed by mental action that involves no physical force upon the object. A number of gifted people exist who seem to be able to effect physical changes without physical contact with the object.

For example, Ingo Swan, a resident of New York, has undergone extensive scientific testing while he raised a thermistor a small amount through mental action alone.[1] Nina Kulagina, a resident of Russia, is able to move objects at a distance with only mental action.[2] Many people, both children and adults, seem to have the ability to bend metal without touching it.[3] Sometimes the strips of metal are sealed in glass test tubes to ensure that no actual touching can occur.[4] No satisfactory explanation for this kind of action has yet been proposed.

I have never had a convincing experience that might possibly fall into this category.

Recurrent Spontaneous Psychokinesis

Recurrent spontaneous psychokinesis (RSPK) describes a phenomenon

---

1. G.R. Schmeidler, "PK Effects Upon Continuously Recorded Temperature," *Journal of the American Society for Psychical Research,* Vol. 67, No. 4, October 1973, 325–40.
2. J.G. Pratt, and H.H. Keil, "Firsthand Observations of Nina S. Kulagina Suggestive of PK Upon Static Objects," *Journal of the American Society for Psychical Research,* October 1973, 381–90.
3. John Hasted, *The Metal Benders*, Routledge and Kegan Paul, Boston, 1981.
4. Robert Tocquet, "Les Expériences Que J'ai Réalisées avec J.P. Girard," *Psi, La Grande Revue Internationale du Surnaturel Face à la Science*, 151, Boulevard Haussmann, Paris, France, Septembre-Octobre 1977, 20-25.

that entails repeated spontaneous movements of objects in a particular locale without any visible means of locomotion. In RSPK, objects may repeatedly either "fall" off desks, bookshelves, shop displays, or tables or seem to be "thrown" by some unseen force.

Until recently this category has been unfortunately named. It is the phenomenon that has been called by the German word *poltergeist*, meaning "a noisy ghost." The use of such a term seems to imply that there is a ghost behind such activity, but it is not necessary to believe in such a worldview to study this phenomenon. Consequently, the category has been relabeled recurrent spontaneous psychokinesis, or RSPK. However, the older term is still in use in many places.

Several years ago when I was teaching a class on the subject of this book and had arrived at the topic of RSPK, I had explained that some parapsychologists believe there is frequently a teenager involved when these activities take place.[5] The teenagers who have been studied seem to harbor a great amount of unexpressed hostility and frustration. While they are ostensibly unaware of being involved in the RSPK destructive activity, the theory states that unconsciously they are exerting psychokinetic energy upon their environment to express that hostility or frustration.[6]

One of my students stated that, when she was a teenager, her parents were going through a divorce and that she felt full of a lot of unexpressed anger. She was frequently sent next door to do her homework in the library of a neighbor's house. Finally, she refused to go into that room again because books kept jumping off the shelves when she was in the room alone, and it frightened her too much.

Within two or three seconds after having told that story, two large, heavy notebooks fell off the bookshelf behind her and about fourteen feet to her left. Two of the four walls of my office, where we were holding the class, are covered with bookshelves full of books. I had been in the same office for over seven years at that time, and never had a book fall off my shelves. It is, of course, conceivable that such an event was sheer coincidence. However, if the chances were calculated for such an event's happening just at the same time that a similar

---

5. However, see Karlis Osis, and Donna McCormick, "A Poltergeist Case Without an Identifiable Living Agent," *Journal of the American Society for Psychical Research*, January 1982, Vol. 76, No. 1, 23–51.

6. However, see Alfonso Martinez-Taboas, "An Appraisal of the Role of Aggression and the Central Nervous System in RSPK Agents," *Journal of the American Society for Psychical Research*, January 1984, Vol. 78, No. 1, 55–69.

event was being described, the odds would obviously be tremendously high. If, by definition, RSPK activity is impossible, then one must conclude that it was coincidence. If, however, one at least tentatively accepts that category as one that has a correspondence to reality, then that event is an appropriate candidate for fitting into such a category.

During the writing of this book a somewhat similar experience happened to me. I got up at five o'clock one Saturday morning and began working at my portable computer. I had recently installed a new version of my word processor program, but it wasn't working properly. I spent almost five hours being terribly frustrated because it would not do what I wanted it to do.

Around 11:00 A.M. I knew I had to go out and buy groceries, so I went to the market. I got a shopping cart and went to the shelves to pick up some crackers. When I had the crackers in my hand, I dropped them into the cart from a height of about one and a half feet. They made a loud noise, as if I had thrown them, but I had only let them drop. A woman in front of me turned around and looked at me as if to say, "What's the matter with you?" She seemed to be thinking that I had thrown the crackers into the cart in anger. (So far, there is nothing inexplicable about this event. I was upset enough to have thrown the crackers, but I hadn't.)

I went further down the aisle to the shelves to get a jar of jam. I reached up and took one jar, but another jar to my left (about two feet away) fell onto the floor and broke. I was embarrassed and decided to go report it so that it could be cleaned up. (There is nothing inexplicable about this event. In reaching for the first jar, the other jar could have fallen off the shelf because of jostling.)

Then, as I turned the corner with my cart, a bottle of mineral water seemed to jump off the shelf onto the floor. Fortunately, the plastic bottle didn't break, so I just put it back on the shelf, thinking that I had not seen the cart knock it onto the floor. I thought to myself, "Oh, I wonder if it is going to be one of those 'awful' days where everything goes wrong!" (There is still nothing completely inexplicable about this event, though it was more puzzling than the others.)

Finally, I went further into the store and began to look for canned goods. I found what I wanted, but when I moved my hand to pick up the can I wanted to buy, I saw another can (about one foot away) begin to "dance" on top of the other cans. It moved rapidly from side to side with the top going from left to right and back again repeatedly, tapping the bottom edges of the can as if it were dancing. It really startled me, and I reached out and grabbed it to make it stop doing that. It offered no resistance, and I was able to set it back on top of the other cans.

I tried to think what would have made that happen. There had been no sensible vibration that I could feel from the floor. The can was not in a precarious position. There was no handy explanation for what had happened, but I was convinced that if I had not reached up and made it stop dancing, it would have fallen off the stack of cans onto the floor. I didn't want any more accidents to happen, so I left the store and tried to get hold of my emotions. It took me a long time to settle down and return to a normal state.

Each one of these events (except the last one) could have a quite normal explanation. But the cluster of events and my intense feeling of frustration seemed to be more than coincidence.

Paranormal Healing

In today's society, people normally think of medical doctors as physical healers of the body and psychiatrists as mental healers of the mind, but the distinction between the two branches has become less and less sharp. Science has become more aware of the effect that the mind can have over physical illness, and the effect that the body can have over mental illness has become more and more recognized. Medical doctors who have relied most heavily on medicine now are beginning to pay serious attention to the emotional condition of their patients. Psychiatrists who have relied primarily on "talk therapy" now find themselves using medicines more and more.

Both medical doctors and psychiatrists are solidly within the scientific establishment. But there have always been people who see themselves as healers but who do not fit into the scientific establishment so well. They have gone by various names in the past: faith healers, spiritual healers, psychic healers, etc. I have not had any personal experience with such healers, but many patients claim they have been healed by them.

Parapsychologists have studied a large number of these healers. They have categorized this phenomenon under the heading of psychokinesis since it appears to involve a change in the physical state of a *living* entity accomplished by mental action alone. Just as the parapsychologists study the phenomenon of mediumship without having to accept the explanation of the medium as to what is actually happening, parapsychologists also study the phenomenon of healing without necessarily accepting the presuppositions of the healer as to why the healing takes place. (The religious or occult presuppositions of the healer are set aside in order to study the phenomenon itself.)

Since suggestibility in humans can play a large part in healing, a number of experiments have been carried out that try to avoid this possibility. During the 1950s, parapsychologists began to experiment on living organisms that could not be influenced by suggestibility. One of the first of such experiments was done on paramecia. It showed that psychokinesis seemed to have been involved in affecting the paramecia.[7] Some time later a person who claimed to be a healer attempted successfully to influence the growth of seedlings.[8] Studies were also conducted on plants to see if mental concentration could influence activity as measured by a polygraph. The results were positive.[9] Experiments were also done on fungal plant parasites to see if a healer could inhibit the growth of the fungus. The fungus that was concentrated on by the healer grew less than the controls.[10] Such experiments have continued on nonhuman living organisms with positive results to the present time.[11]

Studies of brain wave activity have also been conducted on healers who are treating human patients. One interesting observation is that as the healer begins to work, a particular brain wave pattern begins to develop in the healer. As time goes on, the brain wave pattern begins to be induced into the patient as well.[12] This phenomenon does not occur when a "nonhealer" is instructed to do the same external things as the healer but does not attempt any alteration of consciousness.

Dr. Dolores Krieger, professor of nursing at New York University, teaches nurses to use what she has called "the therapeutic touch" on patients. This is a form of "laying on of hands" that involves altering

7. N. Richmond, "Two Series of PK Tests on Paramecia," *Journal of the American Society for Psychical Research*, 1952, 36, 577–88.

8. Bernard Grad, "A Telekinetic Effect on Plant Growth, I," in *International Journal of Parapsychology*, 1963 (5), 117–33, and "A Telekinetic Effect on Plant Growth, II," in *International Journal of Parapsychology*, 1964 (6), 473–98.

9. Robert Brier, "PK Effect on a Plant-Polygraph System," in *Progress in Parapsychology*, ed. J.B. Rhine, Parapsychology Press, Durham, N.C., 1971, 102–17.

10. Jean Barry, "Retarding Fungus Growth by PK," in *Progress in Parapsychology*, ed. Rhine, 118–21.

11. Carroll B. Nash, "Test of Psychokinetic Control of Bacterial Mutation," *Journal of the Society for Psychical Research*, April 1984, Vol. 78, No. 2, 145–50.

12. Maxwell Cade says that virtually all healers exhibit a distinctive brain wave pattern when "sending healing energy." Rose Gladden, a British healer, exhibited this pattern on closed-circuit television to four hundred viewers. The pattern was induced into the patient as the healing session progressed. Reported in *Brain Mind Bulletin*, (September 5, 1977): 2.

the state of consciousness of the healer and ultimately of the patient as well.[13] Dr. Krieger teaches this effective technique to nurses whose theological convictions range from very devout to atheistic, but these convictions do not seem to influence the effectiveness of the healing. The therapeutic touch is used in addition to regular medical techniques rather than in place of them. The effect seems to encourage the natural healing capacities of the body to work more effectively.

Discussion of Paranormality

In the last two chapters I have discussed events that might be classified as "paranormal" events. The categories themselves seem to have a certain usefulness even if they eventually prove to be inadequate as categories.

It is quite obvious that even though people in the Bible would never have used terms like the ones parapsychologists use, they, nevertheless, believed in the reality of what the parapsychologists would call paranormal events, both extrasensory and psychokinetic events. This is not to be taken as evidence either for or against the actual existence of such events. Various cultures in various parts of the world have held beliefs about what would be called paranormal events, but that is an anthropological observation rather than a collection of evidence for proof that paranormal events occur.[14] On the other hand, the reality of their thinking that such events could occur is a psychological fact that is beyond dispute.

Now, having looked at the research being done in physiology, psychology, and parapsychology, it is possible to study with a new perspective both the visionary process itself and other phenomena found in biblical literature.

---

13. Dolores Krieger, *The Therapeutic Touch: How to Use Your Hands to Help or to Heal,* Prentice Hall, New York, 1979.
14. See Thomas W. Overholt, *Prophecy in Cross-Cultural Perspective,* Scholars Press, Atlanta, Ga., 1986, for comparisons of the biblical prophets with their anthropological equivalents in the Americas, the Arctic, Africa, India, and the Pacific.

Part Four: The Study of Biblical Literature

5. Examples from Prophetic Literature

The Bible contains a very large amount of literature, much of it seeming to be prophetic material. It is important to be certain that the data used for the study of prophecy are actually prophetic literature and not something else. There are many passages in the Bible that at first glance seem to deal directly with what appears to be the phenomenon of prophecy, but upon closer inspection a number of these instances cannot be used for such a study.

Inappropriate Examples

Material that seems to be a first-hand report of a prophetic event has to be examined in the light of modern critical scholarship. When the literature of the Bible is investigated in the same manner by which any other ancient literature is investigated, questions must be asked concerning the author, the date of composition, the place of writing, the sources used by the author, the intentions lying behind the literature, the historical context in which it arose, etc. Frequently, passages that seem to give data for the study of the prophetic experience turn out to have been written at such a distance from the time when they were supposed to have happened that they can only be used to make conclusions about the *author's* assumptions concerning prophecy, rather than the *prophet's* descriptions of his own experiences. Such passages only prove that the ancient Near Eastern world believed prophecy to exist as an institution in their culture. Unfortunately, this conclusion is of no help, since that fact has never been doubted.

Furthermore, material that is at first sight prophetic in nature may upon closer inspection turn out to be apocalyptic. Apocalyptic literature arose sometime after the fifth century B.C. when prophecy as an institution in Israel was considered to be dead.[1] Under the influence

---

1. Michael A. Knibb, "Prophecy and the Emergence of the Jewish Apocalypses," in *Israel's Prophetic Tradition,* ed. Richard Coggins, Anthony Phillips, and Michael Knibb, (New York: Cambridge University Press, 1982), 155–80.

of Persian thought-forms, the writers of this literature attempted to copy the visionary style of the older prophetic literature in order to secure an audience. In some cases they set the time of their narrative back into previous historical periods, and by interpreting the "prophetic" dreams of certain characters in the narrative, they could "predict" through the mysterious symbolism of the dreams the various periods of history that had intervened, up to and including events transpiring in their own day.

The best example in the Old Testament of this kind of writing is to be found in the book of Daniel.[2] For example, Daniel 7 purports to be a dream that Daniel dreamed during the period of Nebuchadrezzar (sixth century B.C.) that predicts history for the next 450 years. However, most critical scholars date the writing of this book to the second century B.C. for several reasons. In the first place, a large portion of the Book of Daniel is written, not in Hebrew, but in a dialect of Aramaic that cannot be earlier than the third century B.C., perhaps as late as the second century B.C. The presence of Greek words also points to an age after the conquests of Alexander the Great.[3] The visions themselves show a rather vague knowledge of historical events of the Babylonian and Persian periods, but the details get more and more accurate as they approach the Greek period up to and including the earlier part of the reign of Antiochus Epiphanes in the second century B.C. These facts suggest a date some time before 164 B.C. for the writing of this book. The only element of genuine prediction in the book is the prediction of Antiochus Epiphanes's death and the establishment of the kingdom of God that was to follow. Everything else is history viewed in retrospect.[4]

---

2. See Daniel 7, especially, for this kind of dream interpretation.

3. Norman W. Porteous, *Daniel: A Commentary*, SCM Press, London, 1965, 20.

4. Ibid., 13. Daniel is to be seen as a sample of the class of apocalypse like "Enoch, the Testaments of the Twelve Patriarchs, Baruch, the Assumption of Moses, II Esdras and even Christian apocalypses like the Ascension of Isaiah and the Book of Revelation (this last-named book, however, breaking with the habit of pseudonymity)," (p. 14). See also Thomas S. Kepler, *Dreams of the Future: Daniel and Revelation*, Abingdon Press, New York, 1963; Louis F. Hartman, "Book of Daniel," in *The Anchor Bible*, Doubleday, Garden City, N.Y., 1977; Raymond Hammer, "Book of Daniel," in *The Cambridge Bible Commentary*, Cambridge University Press, New York, 1976; John J. Collins, *The Apocalyptic Vision of the Book of Daniel*, (Missoula, Mont.: Scholars Press for Harvard Semitic Museum, 1977); André Lacocque, *The Book of Daniel*, John Knox Press, Atlanta, 1979; James M. Efird, *Daniel and Revelation: A Study of Two Extraordinary Visions*, Judson Press, Valley Forge, Pa., 1978.

The New Testament Book of Revelation is also apocalyptic literature *par excellence*. Most scholars believe it to be a conscious literary creation intended to contain "dreamlike elements" similar to the genuine prophetic passages in the period before the fifth century B.C. (when prophecy was believed to have ceased). It is not viewed as a first-person account of a subjective experience that actually happened to the narrator and is interpreted by him after the experience has occurred.

Sometimes readers of the Book of Revelation get so absorbed with the presupposition that the book predicts small details of history that will occur in the far future that they are driven to extremes of interpretation. For example, the mysterious number of the beast, *666* (Rev. 13:18), was interpreted to mean "Hitler" during World War II.[5] Throughout history, various people have been identified with this mysterious number when it seemed appropriate to the interpreter: Muhammad, Napoleon, Luther, Kaiser Wilhelm, Mussolini, Pope Benedict IX, and even the World Council of Churches![6]

While both Daniel and Revelation are of enormous importance for the study of apocalyptic literature, they are not appropriate data for the study of the phenomenon of prophecy.[7]

There are also a few passages outside of apocalyptic literature that are, without question, examples of *vaticinium ex eventu*, that is, the creation of a prophecy to predict an event that has already taken place. For example, 1 Kings 13:1–32 tells of a prophet who predicts that a king named Josiah will destroy the altar that Jeroboam I set up at Bethel. In fact, three centuries later, a king named Josiah *did* indeed destroy that altar (2 Kings 23:15–18), but the body of literature in which both these episodes appear was written down *after* both "events." The altar was destroyed and the prophecy was created to justify that destruction. Thus, the passage is of no use in the study of prophetic experience.

Appropriate Examples

In spite of the existence of such inappropriate data for the study of

---

5. If A is assigned a numerical value of 100, B = 101, C = 102, D = 103, etc., the total of the numerical values of the letters in the name *Hitler* comes to 666. Consequently, Hitler must be the beast in Revelation. Kepler, *Dreams of the Future*, 65.

6. Ibid.

7. For further study of the Book of Revelation, see G.B. Caird, *The Revelation of St. John the Divine*, Black's New Testament Commentaries, A. & C. Black, London, 1984; J. Massyngberde Ford, "Revelation: Introduction, Translation and Commentary," in *The Anchor Bible*, Doubleday, Garden City, N.Y. 1975.

prophecy in the Bible, one must not be led to conclude that the Bible contains only such material. There still remains a very large amount of valuable data quite pertinent to the study of genuinely prophetic material and that were written down much nearer the time when the experience occurred.

However, we must be careful in using the word *prophetic* in a biblical context. Prophecy is not to be equated with precognition or with the prediction of future events. When applied to the phenomenon found in the Bible, it has a much broader meaning than that. In recent decades, it became fashionable in scholarly circles concerned with the study of biblical prophecy to say that the prophets in the Bible were "forthtellers" as opposed to "foretellers." Such a statement was felt to be needed as a kind of counterbalance to the assertions of avid religious fanatics who insisted upon seeing the fulfillment of biblical prophecy in such modern events as nuclear disasters, race riots, the rise of communism, etc. Insofar as such a counterbalance was provided by this catch phrase, it was valuable. But, as is the case with any catch phrase, there is more to it than that. The prophets were indeed primarily concerned, not with predicting what was going to happen in the future, but with proclaiming the judgment of God upon the present. However, the fact remains that they did, with some frequency, make predictions that were fulfilled, not in some unseen and distant future, but in their own day. By failing to deal with this aspect of the institution of prophecy, scholars have not dealt with the phenomenon of biblical prophecy in its entirety.

The study of the predictive aspect of biblical prophecy is a relatively neglected area. Perhaps one of the reasons it has been neglected is that, until fairly recent years, no discipline seemed to offer very helpful categories for such a study. However, recent physiological, psychological, and parapsychological research does seem to offer seminal concepts directly related to this aspect of the Bible.[8]

The prophetic literature in the Bible is so vast that one must deal only with particular aspects of that literature. This study shall be limited to examples from the visionary and auditory experiences so plentiful in these writings. The various categories suggested by this recent research should help us to understand these experiences more clearly.

---

8. From the theological point of view, such a study would be concerned with the psychology of revelation; from the scientific point of view, such a study would be concerned with the psychology of religious phenomena.

Mode I Thought in Prophecy

If one assumes that the categories that describe hemispheric specialization have some validity, then it ought to be possible to determine if they shed any light upon the prophetic literature of the Bible. However, rather than imply any permanent commitment to the functions of a particular hemisphere, I (along with Braud *et al.*)[9] will use the term *Mode I* when referring to the functions usually associated with the hemisphere that employs Primary Process thought (the nondominant, analogical hemisphere) and *Mode II* when referring to the functions usually associated with the hemisphere that employs Secondary Process thought (the dominant, logical hemisphere). I will assume, then, that the brain functions upon a principle of bimodal consciousness.[10]

I must also make the assumption that, since the Bible is a written document, whatever Mode I experiences are described in that document will be described ultimately in a Mode II (that is, written) form. This fact implies some Mode II "polishing" and editing of the material to make it suitable for Mode II use. This is true, however, of the verbalization of any experience that has originally been one of a primarily nonverbal nature (the reporting of a dream, for instance).

When one examines these categories, it becomes obvious that prophets, when they are being prophetic, think primarily in a Mode I fashion. Mode II thought is much more akin to the way philosophers' minds work when they are thinking philosophically.[11] Prophets receive holistic visions and auditions in the form of visual and verbal imagery, whereas philosophers think in the analytical and linear fashion. As helpful as such a contrast is, however, one must be reminded of the fact that neither the philosopher nor the prophet has had split-brain surgery. Their cerebral cortices are still joined by corpus callosa, and thus each hemisphere is able to work in conjunction with, not in isolation from, the other. The prophet is able to speak in a logical and analytical fashion just as the philosopher is able to dream dreams. But when the prophet is being prophetic or the philosopher is thinking

---

9. W.G. Braud, G. Smith, F. Andrew, and S. Willis, "Psychokinetic Influences on Random Number Generators During Evocation of 'Analytic' versus 'Non-Analytic' Modes of Processing Information," *Research in Parapsychology* (1975): 85.

10. Arthur Deikman, "Bimodal Consciousness," *Archives of General Psychiatry*, 25 (December 1971): 481–89.

11. J. Lindblom, *Prophecy in Ancient Israel* (Philadelphia: Fortress Press, 1963), 2.

philosophically, each may be understood to be using one mode of the bimodal consciousness more than the other. It is largely a matter of preponderance. This physiological research has given us cause to suspect that certain dichotomies may have an anatomical basis. It enables us to look at the prophetic mode of thought as an entity that may have some anatomical correlate.

REM Visions and Auditions

Two categories discussed in part 2, REM dreams and hypnagogic dreams, seem to be immediately relevant to the visions and auditions of the prophets. Unfortunately, the biblical accounts of these experiences are not recorded primarily for the purpose of providing psychological data to be used for the study of altered states of consciousness. As a consequence one must raise the question as to what the actual mental states of prophets were when they experienced these visions.

In the case of REM-like visions, it is not necessary to decide whether the visions are actually something that the prophets saw in their physical environment as opposed to something that is a product of Mode I thinking. The visions contain too many unearthly and dreamlike elements to be taken for the ordinary observations of everyday life. But whether they are to be understood as visions seen while wide awake or as dreams experienced during sleep is not so easy to decide.

A number of scholars have suggested that the prophets received their visions in the form of dreams.[12] In fact, Jeremiah once states, after speaking of a revelation from the Lord, "Thereupon I awoke and looked, and my sleep was pleasant to me" (Jer. 31:26, RSV). But to understand all of these experiences as dreams occurring during sleep seems to be too simple a solution—especially when it is obvious that psychotics are able to have wide-awake hallucinations that are obviously Primary Process, Mode I, productions. However, the term *hallucination* has a pejorative quality that implies mental illness to most people, whereas there is little evidence that the classical prophets suffered from psychosis.[13]

---

12. Num. 12:6 (RSV) states, "If there is a prophet among you, I the LORD make myself known to him in a vision, I speak with him in a dream." See also I. Mendelsohn, s.v. "dream, dreamer," *Interpreter's Dictionary of the Bible,* (1962).

13. The possible exception is Ezekiel, but that evidence is ambiguous. See E.C. Broome, "Ezekiel's Abnormal Personality," *Journal of Biblical Literature,* 65 (1946): 277ff.; Harold Knight, "The Personality of Ezekiel: Priest or Prophet?" *Expository Times,* 61 (1943): 115ff.; and Kelvin van Nuys, "Evaluating the Pathological in Prophetic Experience (Particularly in Ezekiel)," *Journal of Bible and Religion,* 21 (1953): 244–51.

The prophetic literature in the Bible is full of REM-like visions, and only a single example is necessary for illustration. Ezek. 37:1–14 contains the vision of the valley of dry bones. The prophet begins by stating, significantly, that "the hand of the Lord was upon me. . . ." This phrase is fairly common in prophetic literature, and it seems to be intended to indicate the nonvolitional ecstatic nature of the altered state of consciousness that accompanies such visions.[14] The vision itself takes place during the Exile of the Jews in Babylon in the sixth century B.C. The people have been taken away from their homeland by the Babylonians, and they do not know if they will ever be allowed to return home again. In this vision, Ezekiel sees a valley full of dry bones, and he is told to prophesy to these bones. When he does so, they begin to be connected to each other and are gradually clothed with sinews and flesh and skin—but they have no "breath." Then he is told to prophesy to the four "winds," and as he does so, "breath" enters the corpses and they become a great and living army. The vision is then interpreted to mean that Israel as a people has died and has been buried in the Exile, but that they will be brought up out of their Babylonian grave, given a new "spirit," and returned to their own land. The Hebrew language uses the same word for "breath," "wind," and "spirit," (*ruach*). Such by-play on the connotation of a word and such use of visual metaphor is typical both of the REM-type visionary experiences of the prophets and of ordinary dreams.[15] The dreamlike quality of this Mode I type of vision is quite evident. When a reader is confronted with this passage for the first time, that reader sees it in the form of literature. But it is important to understand this, not as a conscious literary device constructed to achieve a certain effect (as in apocalyptic literature), but as the verbalization of what must have been in origin a subjective experience that was predominantly visual. Thus, whether one understands visions to occur while sleeping or while awake, they speak the same language as dreams and have the same "grammar" and "syntax" as dreams.

Hypnagogic Visions and Auditions

The question concerning the state of consciousness of the recipient of hypnagogic visions and auditions (as opposed to REM-like visions and

14. J. Lindblom, *Prophecy in Ancient Israel* (Philadelphia: Fortress Press, 1963), 45, 58, and especially 134f.
15. Of interest in this respect is Robert B. Chisholm, Jr., "Wordplay in the Eighth-Century Prophets, *Bibliotheca Sacra*, 144 (January-March 1987): 44–52.

auditions) may not be quite so complex. Since such brief but vivid experiences occur to modern people most frequently in the twilight zone between waking and sleeping, it is reasonable to assume that this is also the state of consciousness in which the prophets had their hypnagogic experiences. But whether that state was reached *accidentally* as they were drifting off to sleep or *intentionally* as they were delaying the onset of sleep (as in the practice of meditation), we cannot know for sure. Both are possible, and both may have happened at various points in the prophet's development. In either case the "chatter" of thoughts characteristic of Mode II mentation has been stilled enough to give access to the mental processes of Mode I thought.

While most prophetic visions in the Bible seem to be of the REM type, there is another group of prophetic experiences that seems to fall more naturally into this category of hypnagogic imagery. In contrast to the REM-type visions, they are quite brief; they have no lengthy dreamlike plots; they are predominantly visual in nature; the prophets themselves seem to have taken the role of observers rather than performers in the scene. The images themselves are not intrinsically "religious," that is, they do not necessarily have anything to do with official religion. They are, on the whole, images of fairly ordinary things—locusts forming,[16] flames of fire,[17] a plumb line by a wall,[18] a basket of summer fruit,[19] a branch of an almond tree,[20] a boiling pot facing from the north,[21] two baskets of figs in front of the Temple.[22] If one includes Jesus with those in the Bible who have had the prophetic type of experience (as Matt. 13:57; 21:11; and Mark 6:4 seem to do), his visionary experiences, like those of the Old Testament prophets, may also contain images we would classify as hypnagogic. For instance, in the narrative describing the temptations in the wilderness (Luke 4:1–13), Jesus has three visionary experiences, one of which contains a vision of "all the kingdoms of the world" (shown to him, significantly, "in a moment of time"—Luke 4:5).

In most of these instances the images themselves are so ordinary that some commentators have suggested that the individuals were actually seeing things in their immediate physical environment. However, not

---

16. Amos 7:1–3.
17. Amos 7:4–6.
18. Amos 7:7–9.
19. Amos 8:1–3.
20. Jer. 1:11–12.
21. Jer. 1:13–19.
22. Jeremiah 24.

all of these images are that ordinary. For instance, in Amos's experience (Amos 7:7–9) the Lord himself is holding the plumb line with his own hand beside the wall. That is not the kind of scene one normally sees when passing a construction site. Nor are "all the kingdoms of the world" shown to a person in any way but a visionary way. Consequently, a visionary explanation seems such more satisfactory.

In each of these Old and New Testament visions, the "manifest content" is open to a large number of analogical interpretations. But in every case, the immediate authors of the visions (leaving the question of the "ultimate" author on one side) can be thought of as the prophets themselves. It is *their* Mode I production, and *they* are the expert in its interpretation.[23] Accordingly, the written accounts of such biblical visions usually contain a few sentences that explain how the prophet arrives at the meaning[24] of the Mode I vision in Mode II terms. Sometimes this process is described as a kind of conversation between the prophet and God (as in the instances quoted above from the Old Testament)[25] or between the prophet and the devil (in the case of the visions during the temptations in the wilderness in the New Testament). In other words, the meaning of the manifest content is not always immediately obvious. It requires some kind of associative process that works by analogical, nonlinear reasoning to arrive at the meaning of the image.

In some cases a pun or *double entendre* lies hidden beneath our English translation of the biblical text. For example, when Amos has the vision of a basket of "summer fruit" (*qāyits* in Hebrew), he interprets the meaning of the vision to be that the "end" of Israel is inevitable ("end" in Hebrew is *qēts*). Jeremiah sees a vision of an "almond" branch (*shāqed* in Hebrew), which he interprets to be a statement concerning the "watching" of the Lord over Israel ("watching" in Hebrew is *shōqed*).

---

23. That such visions can be used by God for his own purposes is obvious, but such a subject belongs to a specifically theological discussion.
24. The "meaning" of a prophetic passage is a very complex issue: see John F.A. Sawyer, "A Change of Emphasis in the Study of the Prophets," *Israel's Prophetic Tradition*, ed. Richard Coggins, Anthony Phillips, and Michael Knibb, (New York: Cambridge University Press, 1982), 233–49.
25. E.g., " 'Amos, what do you see?' And I said, 'A plumb line' " (Amos 7:8); " 'Amos, what do you see?' And I said, 'A basket of summer fruit' " (Amos 8:2); " 'Jeremiah, what do you see?' And I said, 'I see a rod of almond' " (Jer. 1:11); "It was deep enough to swim in, a river that could not be passed through. And he said to me, 'Son of man, have you seen this?' " (Ezek. 47:6).

However, puns are not always involved. Sometimes the image is understood as a visual metaphor to be treated analogically. When Amos sees the Lord holding a plumb line beside a wall (Amos 7:7–9), he interprets this image to mean that Israel's moral deviation from uprightness is going to bring about a great collapse, just as an untrue wall that can be shown by a plumb line to deviate from uprightness will inevitably fall over. In each instance the method of analogical interpretation used by the prophet is remarkably similar to the methods of free association found in the modern psychoanalytical approach to the understanding of dreams. Both such interpretations involve the translation of Mode I (visual or verbal imagery) into Mode II (prosaic) language.

Sometimes, when this psychoanalytic approach to the interpretation of the visual metaphors of hypnagogic imagery is used, it results in fresh insights into the meaning of the passage. To illustrate this, one might look in some detail at the temptations of Jesus as they are described in Luke 4:1–13.

It is necessary to make several assumptions about this passage. The first presupposition is that the three visions as presented in the Lukan text have not been *essentially* modified in their content and that, since the experience is one that occurs in solitude, the original source for the content of the visions is Jesus himself.

The second presupposition is that it is necessary to take the human nature of Jesus very seriously, just as the historic creeds of the Church have done. Being "fully human" (as well as "fully divine") means that his human nature is genuine, not a pretense. So, it is important to understand his mind in a truly human fashion.

The third presupposition is that if his mind is really human, then whatever is learned about our human minds can be applied to his human mind.

The three visions that Jesus had in the wilderness of Judaea after his baptism are short enough to be called hypnagogic visions. If hypnagogic images frequently are attempts to solve problems that the logical mind has been unable to solve, what problem is it that he is facing at this point?

He has just come from a tremendously important experience for him —his baptism in the Jordan by John. He has not yet begun his ministry. He goes into the wilderness to think through the implications of this experience. The question under consideration most likely is, What form is my ministry to take? If one remembers that one is looking at the human mind of Jesus, one is looking at a mind that does not see the future in any great detail, any more than other human minds do.

The text says (in the Revised Standard Version), *And Jesus, full of the Holy Spirit, returned from the Jordan, and was led by the Spirit for forty days in the wilderness, tempted by the devil. And he ate nothing in those days* (so obviously he was fasting—a process that is known to make access to the unconscious easier); *and when they were ended he was hungry* (it does not say he was thirsty; in fact, no human being can go for any great length of time without water. Fasting can go on for extremely long periods of time as long as water is available. There are several springs in the wilderness of Judaea between Jerusalem and Jericho, so water would not have been a serious problem). *The devil said to him, "If you are the Son of God, command this stone to become bread." And Jesus answered him, "It is written, 'Man shall not live by bread alone.' "* (Sometimes the physical needs of the visionary are incorporated into the vision itself.)[26]

In the dry creek beds (wadis) of that desert area are many stones that resemble the shape of the bread of those days. It is not difficult to imagine Jesus sitting in the shade of a massive rock, almost dozing off, being hungry, incorporating the image of bread into a hypnagogic image that was used to try to solve the problem, How do I carry out my ministry?

Why not feed people? Hunger was just as much a real problem then as it is now. Feeding the hungry is a noble mission. Give people what they ask for first of all—bread. But Jesus rejects that—not because it is not a good vocation, but because it simply was not good enough. Man lives by more than bread.

And the devil took him up (Where? Up in the sky? Up on a mountain? Or did he go up in his mind's eye and survey the earth as we do sometimes?) *and showed him all the kingdoms of the world in a moment of time* (hypnagogic images are very brief). *And said to him, "To you I will give all this authority and their glory; for it has been delivered to me, and I will give it to whom I will. If you, then, will worship me, it shall all be yours." And Jesus answered him, "It is written, 'You shall worship the Lord your God, and him only shall you serve.' "*

---

26. In Acts 10:9ff., Peter also has what seems to be a hypnagogic vision while he is in a revery on the roof, waiting for lunch to be prepared in the house below. His vision concerns "eating" animals let down in a great sheet from heaven. This vision also deals with seeking a solution to a problem. The answer to the problem has been presented in terms that include the condition of the visionary (hunger).

Jesus' mind pictures all the kingdoms of the world, and the question arises, Can my vocation be to exercise political power? Certainly, Jesus had great potential as a leader, and political power is not bad in itself. It is both effective and good when it is properly used. But is it good enough? Should the thrust of Jesus' ministry be aimed in this direction? After all, if his ancestry went back to David, was it not theoretically possible that he could make an effort to restore the "throne of David" and occupy that throne himself? Surely this option must have crossed his mind.

The first temptation dealt with *physical* needs. Bread is fairly concrete. The second temptation is a little more abstract. It has to do with *social* needs as opposed to physical needs. One is as legitimate as the other, and both are good. The issue really is, Are they good enough?

Two doors have been closed. Then he considers a third option, also in metaphorical form.

And he took him to Jerusalem. The walk to Jerusalem would have taken several hours. But, if we see that as a different kind of journey, a mental journey, it takes no more than a second or two. *And set him on the pinnacle of the temple.* The word for "pinnacle" in Greek is *pterugion*; it means the "tip or extremity of anything." It does not necessarily mean the roof of the Temple itself, and many people today assume that the southeastern corner of the Temple platform built by Herod the Great is intended here. Today when one looks down to the Kidron Valley beneath, it is a dizzying site indeed, and in ancient times before the Romans destroyed that portion of the wall in A.D. 70, it was three times as high.

If this is a hypnagogic vision, and if such visions are clothed in visual metaphors, it is necessary to translate it into ordinary prose to see what really is at issue here. Jesus is encouraged to throw himself down from this pinnacle but not to commit suicide—just the opposite. The biblical texts that follow attempt to show that God will protect people who trust in him: *And (he) said to him, "If you are the Son of God, throw yourself down from here; for it is written, 'He will give his angels charge of you, to guard you,' and 'On their hands they will bear you up, lest you strike your foot against a stone.'"*

What is the meaning of this "leaping out into space" from the pinnacle? Is it an appeal to perform miraculous works that defy gravity? If one takes seriously the assertion that this is visual metaphor, it would be making a mistake to interpret it in such a miraculous way.

Some years ago, after seeing the movie *Superman,* I went to bed and dreamed that I could fly. It was an extremely vivid dream. I was completely free from the earth, completely free from obstructions, free from gravity, free from everything that held me back, free from difficulties, from fear, from injury.

Now, I am well aware that Freud treats such flying dreams differently. But to me it symbolized getting rid of everything that held me down. In the context of the hypnagogic vision of Jesus, leaping out into space like that is metaphorically equivalent to committing yourself totally, holding nothing back. It is a complete giving of one's self.

Is there anyone who is at all "religious" who has not had a period in his or her life when a prayer was uttered something like this: "God, I want to offer you *everything*. I don't want to hold back *anything*. I give you *everything*. I commit myself to you *entirely*. I ask nothing in return, absolutely *nothing* whatsoever—except that you will guarantee that I will not get hurt. Guarantee that you will put your angels in charge of me to guard me, to bear me up so that I won't stumble. That is *all* I ask."

Jesus' first temptation was to supply *physical* needs and to be satisfied with that. The second temptation lay in the area of *social* needs. But the third temptation is the most tempting of all. It doesn't deal with physical or social needs. When interpreted as visual metaphor, it deals with *emotional* needs . . . the need for a feeling of security. One would like to offer one's self completely—holding nothing back. All we ask in return is the assurance that we won't be hurt!

Jesus answered the devil by saying, *It is said, "You shall not tempt the Lord your God"*—the equivalent of saying you must not offer a business deal to God. It is insulting and degrading and takes away the necessity for faith and trust.

Now, if these temptations are seen in this light (the light that a study of human consciousness can throw upon them), the humanity of Jesus seems to take on a reality that we may not have seen before.

There is another genuinely human element to be noted here. Jesus is faced with three solutions to the question, How do I exercise my ministry? Each solution is rejected as flawed. He knows how *not* to exercise his ministry. But there is no final answer to the question, Which specific direction is my ministry to take? If his humanity was genuine, it could be nothing else. No human being knows the future in detail. Jesus came to the same conclusion we come to in such a situation. Visual metaphors can be very helpful in problem solving, but they do not offer detailed blueprints for the future.

As has been noted earlier, most hypnagogic experiences are visual. However, it has been found that approximately one fourth of such hypnagogic experiences may be auditory or kinesthetic in nature.[27] There are many accounts in the Bible of brief auditory experiences. Rabbinic literature has coined the technical term *bath qōl*, "daughter of a voice," to indicate such brief auditions. While there are a number of such experiences recorded in the Bible, each must be studied on its own merits to determine whether it has been mediated over a period of time by oral transmission before it was written down. For example, Samuel's childhood experience of hearing his name called several times during the night (1 Samuel 3) would have been an excellent example of hypnagogic audition if it had come directly from Samuel himself. Instead, the form in which it appears in the Bible at present has resulted from a long period of oral transmission. While it may tell us something about the assumptions of the people who recorded the story, it can hardly be used as direct evidence of an experience had by Samuel himself.

The New Testament has a number of such auditions, but they are frequently combined with visionary elements: at Jesus' baptism—"Thou art my beloved Son; with thee I am well pleased" (Mark 1:11, RSV); at Saul's conversion—"Saul, Saul, why do you persecute me?" (Acts 9:5-6, RSV); at Peter's decision concerning the admission of Gentiles to the Church—"Rise, Peter; kill and eat" (Acts 10:13, RSV); at Paul's decision to preach in Macedonia—"Come over to Macedonia and help us" (Acts 16:9, RSV). Unfortunately, all of these examples have been mediated by oral transmission to a greater or lesser extent and, as a consequence, lose some of their value as first-hand data. But many of them must surely go back to genuine experiences that would be classified as hypnagogic auditions.[28]

Paranormality

When the Bible is examined in terms of the categories of the paranormal, it becomes evident that there is an almost embarrassing abundance of parapsychological riches. Examples of telepathy[29], clairvoyance,[30]

---

27. David Foulkes, *The Psychology of Sleep* (New York: Scribner's Sons, 1966), 125.

28. Some of these auditions have, in all probability, been expanded and polished in order that they be suitably clear for a Mode II type of thinking.

29. Elisha knows the words that the king of Syria speaks in his own bedchamber (2 Kings 6:8-12). Jesus knows about the five husbands of the Samaritan woman (John 4:16-19, 39).

30. Samuel knows where Saul's lost asses are (1 Sam. 9:20).

precognition,[31] mediumship,[32] psychokinesis,[33] and out-of-body experiences abound.[34] But here the data must be chosen with the same caution that was used in the previous sections. The reporting of such events long after they were said to have happened limits their value severely. Such reporting may tell more about the reporter than about the event. On the other hand, there are instances where the data come nearer to being first-hand accounts and which, as a consequence, may merit close attention.

There has never been any question that the ancient world believed in the paranormal—even though they would not have used such a descriptive term. Nor is our purpose in discussing this subject to prove that paranormal events do or do not occur. Rather it is our purpose to see if some of the parapsychological categories currently being investigated can help us to understand the biblical material better.

In other words, people today have experiences that are described in terms of extrasensory perception. These experiences often prove to be quite vivid ones that can make an emotional impact upon the percipient that is not easily forgotten. One does not have to draw a final conclusion about the "reality" of such experiences before studying them as particular psychological syndromes. One does not always have to agree with the explanation of the phenomenon offered by the percipient in order to study the phenomenon itself. Nor must one automatically deny, without examining the evidence, that such an event is possible. A more profitable approach is one that weighs and considers the evidence rather

---

31. Joseph dreams precognitively about his future position (Gen. 37:5-11); he also interprets a dream about the butler's future (Gen. 40:8-13) and one about the famine in Egypt (Gen. 41:1-36). Samuel knows a day before Saul's arrival of his coming (1 Sam. 9:15-17) and knows that Saul will meet certain men when he departs from Samuel (1 Sam. 10:2) and that Saul will himself prophesy when he meets a band of prophets (10:3-9). Jesus knows of his future sufferings (Matt. 16:21; 17:22-23; 20:18-19; 26:2). Jesus saw Nathaniel under a fig tree before he had met him (John 1:47-48). Jesus knows who will betray him (John 13:18-21, 38). Jesus predicts the persecution of his followers (John 16:4).
32. Saul consults a medium at Endor (1 Sam. 28:3-19). Job 4:12-21 sounds as if mediumship is being described.
33. Elijah raises a boy from the dead (1 Kings 17:17-24) as does his successor, Elisha (2 Kings 4:18-37). Elisha causes an axe head to float in the water (2 Kings 6:1-7). The Gospels contain numerous healing miracles by Jesus. Saul receives his sight by the laying on of hands by Ananias (Acts 9:12). A lame man is healed by fixing his attention on Peter (Acts 3:2-8). Many sick are healed by Peter (Acts 5:16; 9:33-34, 37-42). Paul also heals the sick (Acts 14:8-11; 28:8).
34. Elisha goes out "in spirit" and observes his servant Gehazi (2 Kings 5:26).

than one that rushes to accept or reject that evidence because of preconceived ideas.

It must be pointed out, however, that when appropriate biblical accounts that seem to parallel modern parapsychological categories are investigated, the investigation itself ceases to be a parapsychological investigation and becomes a psychological study of the biblical accounts. Parapsychology is concerned with whether or not there is an objectively verifiable paranormal occurrence. Since the events described in the Bible are so distant in both time and space, neither scholars nor parapsychologists have access to objective data that would help to decide such a matter. The investigation, consequently, must be a psychological investigation of the account of what may or may not have originally been a paranormal event.

Precognition

The most obvious example of the application of a parapsychological category to prophetic literature is that of precognition—knowing that an event is going to happen without recourse to ordinary means of knowing. In the eighth century B.C., Amos, Hosea, Isaiah, and Micah did, in fact, predict by means of a large number of Mode I–type visions and auditions the fall of the Northern Kingdom of Israel. During the latter part of the seventh and the early part of the sixth centuries B.C., Jeremiah[35] and Ezekiel[36] did predict, by means of an equally large number of similar visions and auditions, the fall of Judah. These predictions came true.

One might suppose, of course, that the Bible has preserved only those prophecies that did come true. But there are actually a number of instances where the Bible preserves prophecies that never happened. For instance, in the eighth century B.C., Isaiah predicts the destruction and fall of Jerusalem,[37] but when the Assyrians invade a few years later, Jerusalem is *not* taken after all.[38] Jerusalem does not actually fall until

---

35. For an excellent discussion of Jeremiah's visions see, Walther Zimmerli, "Visionary Experience in Jeremiah," in *Israel's Prophetic Tradition*, ed. Richard Coggins, Anthony Phillips, and Michael Knibb (New York: Cambridge University Press, 1982), 95–118.
36. For a discussion of the editing process of the Book of Ezekiel, see R.E. Clements, "The Ezekiel Tradition: Prophecy in a Time of Crisis," in *Israel's Prophetic Tradition*, ed. Coggins, Phillips, and Knibb, 119–36.
37. For example, in Isa. 3:1, 8; 5:3–7, and other places.
38. Isaiah 36–37.

the sixth century B.C.—a century and a quarter later—under the Babylonians. If one accepts *that* event as fulfillment of *Isaiah's* prophecy (made a century and a quarter earlier), the question has to be raised, Where does one draw the line? Theoretically, Jerusalem was eventually bound to fall to some invader at some time or another. It takes no prophet to make that kind of statement. Furthermore, in the sixth century B.C., Ezekiel prophesied that Tyre would fall to Nebuchadrezzar,[39] and although Nebuchadrezzar besieged Tyre for thirteen years, it did *not* fall to him.[40] Ezekiel also prophesied that Egypt would fall to Nebuchadrezzar,[41] but that never happened. In the seventh century B.C., the prophetess Hulda said concerning King Josiah, "Thus says the Lord . . . I will gather you to your fathers, and you shall be gathered to your grave in peace" (2 Kings 22:15-20). And yet, King Josiah is described only twenty-nine verses later as having been killed in battle by Pharaoh Neco.[42]

In other words, even the classical prophets were not thought of as infallible when it came to precognition. And if it is true that Mode I-type (analogical) visions must be interpreted by the prophet in Mode II-type (prosaic) thought, there is always a risk of mistranslation, even though the images are understood to be the prophet's own. The unconscious has never been known for taking great pains to make itself completely clear to the conscious mind.

Furthermore, one must not think of the biblical prophets as a kind of information machine that gives answers upon the insertion of the' right kind of coin. Jeremiah, for instance, was asked to pray to God for guidance by some military officers. He agreed to do so, but it was only after ten days had elapsed that "the word of the LORD came to Jeremiah" (Jer. 42:7, RSV). Evidently, prophets must wait for whatever Mode I responses they are expecting to manifest themselves—whether in dreams or in waking visions and auditions.

It is well known that when people mull over problems consciously for a considerable length of time, the emotional intensity increases when a solution does not seem to appear. Frequently, the "solution" finally does come to them in the form of a dream. It is important, however,

---

39. Ezekiel 26-28.
40. Ezekiel 29:17-18.
41. Ezekiel 29:19.
42. See Robert P. Carroll, *When Prophecy Failed: Cognitive Dissonance in the Prophetic Traditions of the Old Testament* (New York: Seabury Press, 1979), 111-28, for a discussion of this matter.

that the symbolic image that incorporates the working out of the problem is not always to be understood as "the answer."[43]

There are other, even more specific instances, of what seem to be experiences of precognition. For example, at one time Jeremiah (Jer. 27:1–28:17) has a confrontation with a prophet named Hananiah, who disagrees with him on the analysis of the political situation. The argument ends with Jeremiah's prediction that Hananiah would die within that very year. Within two months Hananiah is dead.[44]

The Book of Ezekiel also affords us with other examples that seem to fit into paranormal categories. Ezekiel was evidently in the habit of recording the dates of some of his visions, and in Ezek. 24:1 (RSV) one reads that "in the ninth year, in the tenth month, on the tenth day of the month, the word of the LORD came to me: 'Son of man, write down the name of this day, this very day. The king of Babylon has laid siege to Jerusalem this very day.' " Since Ezekiel himself is in exile in Babylon many miles away, this knowledge seems to have come to him from other than ordinary means. Clairvoyance seems to be implied. Furthermore, he is told by the Lord that his wife is to die soon. He continues: "So I spoke to the people in the morning, and at evening my wife died" (Ezek. 24:18, RSV). Here he seems to be implying precognition. It is further revealed to Ezekiel that when the city of Jerusalem falls, a fugitive will come to him with the news. Until that time, however, he will be afflicted with dumbness.[45] Some time later a man who had escaped from Jerusalem did come to him and did tell him that the city had fallen (Ezek. 33:21–22). But the text goes on to explain that "the hand of the LORD" had been upon Ezekiel the evening before the fugitive came, and his dumbness seems to have been lifted that evening *in anticipation* of the arrival of the news from the fugitive the next day. It is impossible to know whether clairvoyance, telepathy, or precognition is the appropriate category here.

As has been stated above, it is not the purpose of this discussion to attempt to prove the accuracy of these accounts or the genuineness of the paranormal events. The time is too far away from us to do so, even if we tried. But it is quite evident that the relating of such an account

---

43. For example, Jesus' visions in the wilderness were all rejected as answers.
44. Whether or not this account is to be understood as precognition or a kind of "execution by suggestion" is not made clear in the biblical text.
45. This "dumbness" may possibly be some kind of hysterical aphasia. See Moshe Greenberg, "On Ezekiel's Dumbness," *Journal of Biblical Literature* 77 (1958): 101–05.

is intended to convey to the reader that a paranormal event has occurred. Furthermore, they seem to occur when "the hand of the LORD" is upon Ezekiel—that is, when he is in what we would call an altered state of consciousness.[46] If such a state is associated with Mode I mentation and if Mode I mentation seems not to perceive time in a Mode II, sequential manner, then perhaps there is some connection, not yet understood, between paranormal perception and Mode I process.

Out-of-Body Experiences

Probably the most extraordinary category under parapsychological investigation is that of the "out-of-body experiences." As has been stated above, a large number of people have claimed that while in an altered state of consciousness they have had experiences in which they feel that they have entirely left their physical bodies and are able to view things as if they were actually present at great distances from their bodies. In some, though not all, instances, information has been acquired while in this state that seems not to have been available by any ordinary means.

One does not have to look very far before finding biblical examples of this kind of parapsychological category. For example, in the sixth century B.C. before the Temple had been destroyed, Ezekiel (chaps. 8–11) tells of a vision he has when the "hand of the LORD" is upon him. He sees what appears to be a man radiant with brightness who puts forth a hand and takes him by a lock of his head and lifts him up between earth and heaven and brings him to Jerusalem, to the entrance of the gateway of the inner court of the Temple. He is shown the events transpiring there—in this instance, it is pagan worship occurring right on the Temple grounds. He is also a witness to the death of one Pelatiah who is participating in the pagan worship. Finally, Ezekiel is shown the departure of the "glory of the LORD" from the Temple itself— evidently in anticipation of the destruction of that building. Then he is lifted up again and brought back to the exiles in Babylon. The reader of this account is not given any external confirmation of the death of Pelatiah or of the pagan worship that was supposed to be taking place at that moment. So one cannot call this veridical information. But the account certainly fits the category of an out-of-body experience. Even the dreamlike elements (the departure of the "glory of the LORD") are paralleled in modern accounts.

---

46. For a discussion of "ecstasy" as an altered state of consciousness, see Robert R. Wilson, "Prophecy and Ecstasy: A Reexamination," *Journal of Biblical Literature* 98 (1979): 321–37.

In the New Testament, Paul describes a similar experience that contains a number of the same elements. He says,

> I must boast; there is nothing to be gained by it, but I will go on to visions and revelations of the Lord. I know a man in Christ who fourteen years ago was caught up to the third heaven—whether in the body or out of the body I do not know, God knows. And I know that this man was caught up into Paradise—whether in the body or out of the body I do not know, God knows—and he heard things that cannot be told, which man may not utter. On behalf of this man I will boast . . ." (2 Cor. 12:1–5, RSV).

It is significant that when Paul relates this first-person, first-hand account, he puts it in the context of "visions and revelations." An altered state of consciousness seems to be implied in this instance as well.

6. Summary and Conclusions

Research on the lateralized functions of the human brain throws light upon the type of mentation characteristic of the biblical prophets. When experiencing visions, the prophets seem to have thought in what has been called Mode I, Primary Process, analogical mentation.

The research on sleep, dreaming, and meditation suggests that two of the dream categories (REM dreams and hypnagogic dreams) may be appropriate categories for the classification of prophetic visions as well. To classify the brief visions as hypnagogic seems much more satisfactory than to understand them as actually seeing physical objects that have been observed in the immediate environment. To classify the longer visions as either genuine waking visions or as dreams obtained during sleep seems more satisfactory than to restrict them entirely to the category of dreams alone. Prophets had visions. One cannot avoid these mystical experiences by taming them into dreams. There is no need to rationalize them into something more acceptable to the modern matter-of-fact mind. Instead, we can picture the prophet performing genuinely human mentation in a genuinely human manner.

In the minds of some people there may be the suspicion that, when the visionary process is understood in this way, the miraculous element in the biblical narrative is eliminated. But one must be exceedingly careful not to read back into the culture of the biblical world the presuppositions about nature that modern people hold. The ancients did not see nature as a system that ran by well-ordered laws as most moderns see it. Most of them were unaware that such laws might even be formulated. If an event were to happen today that seemed to defy the laws that normally are understood to govern nature, the modern mind might classify that event as "miraculous." But in the ancient biblical world there was not even a word for what moderns mean by "miracle." In Hebrew, the words that come nearest to "miracle" are 'oth (but that word means "a sign"), niphla'oth (and this word means "wonders"), and mopheth (which means "a portent"). In Greek, several words also approximate that meaning, such as dunamis ("a work of power"), *sēmeion* ("a sign"), and *teras* ("a wonder"). But both those who spoke Hebrew and those who spoke Greek believed that many wonderful things in nature were meant by God to signify something (e.g., rainbows, storms, etc.). All nature was under the control of God; there was no set of natural laws that governed the natural order. "Signs," "wonders," "portents," and "works of power" were not necessarily defined as something that defied the natural order of things. They were only created things that pointed back to God in a special way.[1]

Consequently, when the visionary process is seen as something that can be understood within the limits of what God has already created in the human brain and mind, the mystery has certainly not been eliminated. The mystery actually lies in the "equipment" that God has already created to be at his disposal when he wants to reveal himself. The Hebrews might have called the brain itself an *'oth* ("a sign") or an example of one of the many *niphla'oth* ("wonders") that exist in his creation.

Parapsychological categories seem to have value as categories for the study of prophecy. But when one examines biblical data, one is restricted by the very nature of that data to a psychological, as opposed to a parapsychological, study. The passages may well have originally been describing what modern people would call paranormal events, but none of us is now close enough to them to be able to know for sure.[2] It is difficult enough to ascertain whether *contemporary*, seemingly paranormal events are paranormal or whether they may be explained by other means. Consequently, a solution as to whether some of these experiences may be of a truly paranormal nature or not is still far away. In fact, further exploration may help one to see that *paranormal* is just another word for that part of normality that is still not fully understood.

From the beginning, the intention has never been to prove *by use of the Bible* that bimodal consciousness does indeed function as some researchers have described it. That proof must be sought in a contemporary setting under proper scientific controls. Nor has the intention been to prove *by use of the Bible* that there is a distinction between

---

1. For a classic discussion of this issue, see H.W. Robinson, *Inspiration and Revelation in the Old Testament* (Oxford: Clarendon Press, 1946), 34–48.

2. It is important to note that not all prophetic visions and auditions fall into parapsychological categories. For example, Jeremiah's vision of the almond branch (Jer. 1:11–12) is interpreted to mean that God is "watching" over Israel. Such a vision is not paranormal in itself, nor is the interpretation easily put into the categories of clairvoyance, telepathy, or precognition.

REM visionary experience and hypnagogic visionary experience. If those categories are discrete categories that occur in the ordinary human sleep cycle, it will be finally determined by sleep research rather than biblical research. Nor has the intention been to prove *by use of the Bible* that parapsychological events do or do not occur. Such research belongs properly to the scientific investigations of parapsychologists. On the contrary, the purpose has been to examine the categories being used in current research in these three fields to see if they might help us to understand more clearly the minds of those biblical prophets who experienced visions and auditions. And, indeed, they seem to make more sense when seen in this light. The people who had these experiences seem to be much more real when seen in these terms.

One difference, however, is obvious when modern people compare themselves to those prophets. Our dreams are mostly personal, whereas their visions seem to deal in religious terms with broad social, political, and moral issues. No doubt personal matters disturbed the prophets, too, and they had dreams of a private nature that were not relevant to society at large. One never hears of those dreams. But they seem to have been concerned enough over the moral and religious plight of their people to make their visions psychologically understandable. When genuine concern turns the volume and brightness up that high, something is bound to happen.

It seems quite necessary now to avoid the temptation to assume that ancient people spoke in rather extravagant ways, and that modern readers must make allowances for the kind of fanciful expressions they use. To some extent, that assertion remains true. Styles of language do change. But one can also see that the extraordinary experiences that prophets describe are not so unfamiliar to modern people as might at first glance be supposed. Without falling into the subtle trap of literalism, it is important to take the descriptive language of these experiences with the utmost seriousness. That is not to say that one should try to read Mode I language as if it were Mode II language. They are not the same thing. But it is equally important to learn to appreciate Mode I language for what it is—an intelligent and beautiful use of both visual and verbal imagery that, as far as the Bible is concerned, has had the ability to move millions of people throughout the ages in ways that are largely inexplicable in Mode II terms. That is one of the insights that has been gained about the phenomenon of religion itself. Religious experience is primarily a matter of Mode I process. Theology, on the other hand, is largely a matter of rationalizing that experience in Mode II language. And in this particular instance it is vitally important to let the right hand know what the left hand is doing.

Bibliography

Part One: Physiology

Surgery

Anninos, P.A., Argyrakis, P. and Skouras, A. "A Computer Model for Learning Processes and the Role of the Cerebral Commissures" *Biological Cybernetics* 50 (1984): 329–36.

Berlucchi, G. "Cerebral Dominance and Interhemispheric Communication in Normal Man," in *The Neurosciences, Third Study Program*, edited by Schmitt, F.O. and Worden, F.G., Cambridge, Mass.: MIT Press, 1974, 65–69.

Bogen, J.E. "The Other Side of the Brain, I, II, III" *Bulletin of the Los Angeles Neurological Societies* 34 (1969) 3.

Bruell, J.H., and Albee, G.W. "Higher Intellectual Functions in a Patient with Hemispherectomy for Tumors" *Journal of Consulting and Clinical Psychology* 26 (1962): 90–98.

Budzynski, Thomas H. "Brain Lateralization and Biofeedback" in *Brain/Mind and Parapsychology*, edited by Shapin, Betty, and Coly, Lisette, New York: Parapsychology Foundation, 1979, 116–42.

Cook, N.D. "Callosal Inhibition: The Key to the Brain Code." *Behavioral Science* 29 (April 1984): 98–110.

Damasio, A.R., Chui, H.C., Corbett, Jr., and Kassel, N. "Posterior Callosal Section in a Non-epileptic Patient." *Journal of Neurology, Neurosurgery and Psychiatry* 43 (April 1980): 351–56.

Deikman, Arthur "Bimodal Consciousness" *Archives of General Psychiatry* 29 (1966): 329–43.

Dewitt, L.W. "Consciousness, Mind, and Self-implications of Split-brain Studies" *BR J PHIL S* 26 (1): 41.

Dimond, S.J., *The Double Brain* London: Elek, 1974.

Durnford, M., and Kimura, D. "Right Hemisphere Specialization for Depth Perception Reflected in Visual Field Difference" *Nature* 231 (1971): 394–95.

Efron, R. "Temporal Perception, Aphasia and Deja vu" *Brain* 86 (1963): 403–24.

Feher, L. "Double-mind Theory" *American Journal of Psychoanalysis* 33 (1973): 210-13.

Filbey, R.A., and Gazzaniga, Michael. "Splitting the Normal Brain with Reaction Time" *Psychonomic Science* 17 (1969): 335-36.

Galin, David "Implications for Psychiatry of Left and Right Cerebral Specialization; A Neurophysiological Context for Unconscious Processes" *Archives of General Psychiatry* 31 (October 1974): 572-83.

Galin, David, and Ornstein, Robert E. "Hemispheric Specialization and the Duality of Consciousness" *Human Behavior and Brain Function* edited by Widroe, H.J., (Springfield, Ill.: Thomas 1974): 3-23.

Gazzaniga, M.S. et al. "Profiles of Right Hemisphere Language and Speech Following Brain Bisection" *Brain Language* 22 (July 1984): 206-20.

_____. "The Split Brain in Man" *Scientific American* August 1967.

_____. *The Bisected Brain* New York: Appleton-Century-Crofts 1970.

_____. "Cerebral Dominance Viewed as a Decision System" edited by Dimond, S.J., and Beaumont, J.G. in *Hemisphere Function in the Human Brain* (London: Elek, 1974).

_____. "Review of the Split Brain" *Journal of Neurology* 209 (1975): 75-79.

Gazzaniga, M.S., LeDoux, J.E., and Wilson, D.H. "Language, Praxis, and the Right Hemisphere: Clues to Some Mechanisms of Consciousness" *Neurology* 27 (December 1977): 1144-47.

Gazzaniga, M.S., Risse, G.L., Springer, S.P., Clark, E., and Wilson, D.H. "Psychologic and Neurologic Consequences of Partial and Complete Cerebral Commissurotomy" *Neurology* 25 (1975): 10-15.

Gazzaniga, M.S., and Smylie, C.S. "Facial Recognition and Brain Asymmetries: Clues to Underlying Mechanisms" *Annals of Neurology* 13 (May 1983): 536-40.

Gazzaniga, M.S., Smylie, C.S., Baynes, K., Hirst, W., and McCleary, C. "Profiles of Right Hemisphere Language and Speech Following Brain Bisection" *Brain Language* 22 (July 1984): 206-20.

Geschwind, N. "The Anatomical Basis of Hemisphere Differentiation" in *Hemisphere Function in the Human Brain,* edited by Dimond, S.J. and Beaumont, J.G. (London: Elek, 1974).

Greenblatt, S.H., Saunders, R.L., Culver, C.M., and Bogdanowicz, W. "Normal Interhemispheric Visual Transfer with Incomplete Section of the Splenium" *Archives of Neurology* 37 (September 1980): 567–71.

Hecaen, H., and Angelergues, R. "Agnosia for Faces (Prosopagnosia)" *A.M.A. Archives of Neurology* 7 (1962): 92–100.

Humphrey, M.E., and Zangwill, O.L. "Cessation of Dreaming After Brain Injury" *Journal of Neurology, Neurosurgery and Psychiatry* 14 (1951): 322–25.

Joseph, R. "The Neuropsychology of Development Hemispheric Laterality, Limbic Language, and the Origin of Thought" *Journal of Clinical Psychology* 38 (January 1982): 4–33.

Kety, Seymore S. *The Brain* New York: W.H. Freeman 1979.

Kinsbourne, M. "The Cerebral Basis of Lateral Asymmetries in Attention" in *Acta Psychologia* edited by Sanders, (A.F. 33 Attention and Performance III, North Holland Pub., Amsterdam, 1970).

Lee, H. Nakada, I., Veal, J.L., Lin, S., Kwee, I.L. "Transfer of Language Dominance" *Annals of Neurology* 15 (March 1984): 304–07.

Levi-Agresti, J., and Sperry, Robert "Differential Perceptual Capacities in Major and Minor Hemispheres" *Proceedings of the National Academy of Sciences* 61 (1968): 1151.

Levy, J. "Psychobiological Implications of Bilateral Asymmetry" in *Hemisphere Function in the Human Brain* edited by Dimond, S.J., and Beaumont, J.G. (London: Elek 1974).

Lindsay, Robert H., and Norman, Donald A. *Human Information Processing*, New York: Academic Press, 1977, 442.

Martin, A. "A Qualitative Limitation on Visual Transfer Via the Anterior Commissure. Evidence from a Case of Callosal Agenesis" *Brain* 108 (Pt. 1) (March 1985): 43–63.

Milner, Brenda "Brain Mechanisms Suggested by Studies of Temporal Lobes" in *Brain Mechanisms Underlying Speech and Language* edited by Darley, F.L., and Millikan, C.H. (New York: Grune and Stratton, 1965).

_____. "Interhemispheric Differences in the Localization of Psychological Processes in Man" *British Medical Bulletin* 27 (1971): 272–77.

Mosidze, V.M. "Split Brain and the Problem of Interhemispheric Relations" *Zhurnal Vysshei Nervnoi Deiatelnosti Imeni I.P. Pavlova* (Moscow) 28 (November-December 1978): 1164-72.

Nagafuchi, M., Susuki, J. "Auditory Agnosia Due to Incision of Splenium Corporis Callosi" *Acta Oto-laryngologica* 76 (Stockholm 1973): 109-13.

Nebes, R.D. "Hemispheric Specialization in Commissurotomized Man" *Psychological Bulletin* 81 (1974): 1-15.

Ogden, J.A. "Dyslexia in a Right-Handed Patient with a Posterior Lesion of the Right Cerebral Hemisphere" *Neuropsychologia* 22 (1984): 265-80.

Penfield, Wilder *The Mystery of the Mind: A Critical Study of Consciousness and the Human Brain* Princeton, N.J.: Princeton University Press, 1975.

Selnes, O.A. "The Corpus Callosum: Some Anatomical and Functional Considerations with Special Reference to Language" *Brain Language* 1 (1974): 111-39.

Semmes, J. "Hemisphere Specialization: A Possible Clue to Mechanism" *Neuropsychologia* 6 (1968): 11-16.

Sidtis, J.J., Volpe, B.T., Wilson, D.H., Rayport, M., and Gazzaniga, M.S. "Variability in Right Hemisphere Language Function after Callosal Section: Evidence for a Continuum of Generative Capacity" *Journal of Neuroscience* 1 (March 1981): 323-31.

Smith, A. "Non-dominant Hemispherectomy" *Neurology* 19 (1969): 442-45.

_____. "Speech and Other Functions after Left (Dominant) Hemispherectomy" *Journal of Neurology, Neurosurgery and Psychiatry* 29 (1966): 467-71.

Sperry, R.W. "Lateral Specialization of Cerebral Function in the Surgically Separated Hemispheres" in *The Psychophysiology of Thinking* edited by McGuigan, F.J., and Schoonover, R.A. (New York: Academic Press 1973): 209-29.

_____. "Lateral Specialization in the Surgically Separated Hemispheres" in *The Neurosciences, Third Study Program* edited by Schmitt, F.O., and Worden, F.G. (Cambridge, Mass.: MIT Press, 1974): 5-19.

_____. "The Great Cerebral Commissure" *Scientific American* (off-print) 174 (1964): 42-52.

Sperry, R.W., Gazzaniga, M.S., and Bogen, J.E. "Interhemispheric Relationships: The Neocortical Commissures; Syndromes of Hemisphere Disconnection" in *Handbook of Neurology* edited by Vinken, P.J. and Bruyn, G.W. (Amsterdam: North Holland Pub. 1969).

Springer, Sally P., and Deutsch, Georg *Left Brain, Right Brain* Rev. Ed. New York: W.H. Freeman and Co. 1985.

Springer, Sally P., Gazzaniga, M.S. "Dichotic Testing of Partial and Complete Split Brain Subjects" *Neuropsychologia* 13 (1975): 341–46.

Teng, E.L., and Sperry, R.W. "Interhemispheric Rivalry During Simultaneous Bilateral Task Presentation in Commissurotomized Patients" *Cortex* 10 (1974): 111–20.

Terzian, H. "Behavioral and EEG Effects of Intracarotid Sodium Amytal Injection" *Acta Neurochirurgia (Wein)* 12 (1964): 230–39.

Trevarthen, C. "Analysis of Cerebral Activities that Generate and Regulate Consciousness in Commissurotomy Patients" in *Hemisphere Function in the Human Brain* edited by Dimond, S.J., and Beaumont, J.G. (New York: Wiley 1974): 235–63.

————. "Brain Bisymmetry and the Role of the Corpus Callosum in Behavior and Conscious Experience" in *Cerebral Interhemispheric Relations* edited by Cernacek, J., and Podivinsky, F. (Bratislava: Vydatelstva Slovenskej Akademie Vied 1972): 319–33.

Trevarthen, C., and Sperry, R.W. "Perceptual Unity of the Ambient Visual Field in Human Commissurotomy Patients" *Brain* 96 (1973): 547–70.

Volpe, B.T., Sidtis, J.J., Holtzman, J.D., Wilson, D.H., and Gazzaniga, M.S. "Cortical Mechanisms Involved in Praxis: Observations Following Partial and Complete Section of the Corpus Callosum in Man" *Neurology* 32 (June 1982): 645–50.

Yamadori, A., Nagashima, I., and Iamaki, N. "Ideogram Writing in a Disconnection Syndrome" *Brain Language* 19 (July 1983): 346–56.

Zaidel, D., and Sperry, R.W. "Memory Impairment After Commissurotomy in Man" *Brain* 97 (1974): 263–72.

Zangwill, O.L. "Consciousness and the Cerebral Hemispheres" in *Hemisphere Function in the Human Brain* edited by Dimond, S.J., and Wiley, J.G. (New York 1974): 264–78.

Electroencephalography

Dement, William C. *Some Must Watch While Others Must Sleep* San Francisco: W.H. Freeman, 1974.

Foulkes, David *The Psychology of Sleep* New York: Charles Scribner's Sons, 1966.

Galin, David, and Ellis, R. "Asymmetry in Evoked Potentials as an Index of Lateralized Cognitive Processes: Relation to EEG Alpha Asymmetry" *Neuropsychologia* 13 (1975): 45–50.

Galin, David, and Ornstein, Robert E. "Lateralization of Cognitive Mode: an EEG Study" *Psychophysiology* 9 (1972): 412–18.

Hill, D., and Barr, G. *Electroencephalography* Macmillan, 1963.

Jones, Richard M. *The New Psychology of Dreaming* New York: The Viking Press, 1970.

Kooi, Kenneth A. *Fundamentals of Electroencephalography* New York: Harper & Row, 1971.

Lehmann, D., Beeler, G.W., and Fender, D.H., "EEG Responses During the Observation of Stabilized and Normal Retinal Images" *Electroencephalography and Clinical Neurophysiology* 22 (1967): 136–42.

Cerebral Angiography

Osborn, Anne G., with Maack, Julian C., et al. *Introduction to Cerebral Angiography* Hagerstown, Md.: Harper & Row, 1980.

Waddington, Margaret M. *Atlas of Cerebral Angiography with Anatomic Correlation* Boston: Little, Brown, 1974.

Computerized Axial Tomography

Basso, A., Capitani, E., Laiacona, M., and Zanobio, M.E. "Crossed Aphasia: One or More Syndromes?" *Cortex* 21 (March 1985): 25–45.

Bear, Y., Schiff, Y., Saver, J., Greenberg, M., and Freeman, R. "Quantitative Analysis of Cerebral Asymmetries, Fronto-occipital Correlation, Sexual Dimorphism and Association with Handedness" *Archives of Neurology* 43 (June 1986): 598–603.

De Renzi, E. "Prosopagnosia in Two Patients with CT Scan Evidence of Damage Confined to the Right Hemisphere" *Neuropsychologia* 24 (1986): 385–89.

Ferro, J.M., and Martins, I.P. "Neglect in Children" *Annals of Neurology* 15 (March 1984): 281-84.

Koff, E., Maeser, M.H., Pieniadz, J.M., Poundas, H.L., and Levine, H.L. "Computed Tomographic Scan Hemispheric Asymmetries in Right- and Left-Handed Male and Female Subjects" *Archives of Neurology* 43 (May 1986): 487-91.

Henderson, V.W., Maeser, M.H., Weiner, J.M., Pieniadz, J.M., and Chui, H.C. "CT Criteria of Hemisphere Asymmetry Fail to Predict Language Laterality" *Neurology* 34 (August 1984): 1086-89.

Lund, L.; Spliid; P.E.; Andersen, E.; and Bojsen-Miller, M. "Vowel Perception: A Neuroradiological Localization of the Perception of Vowels in the Human Cortex" *Brain Language* 29 (November 1986): 191-211.

Naeser, M.A., and Borod, J.C., "Aphasia in Left-Handers: Lesion Site, Lesion Side, and Hemispheric Asymmetries on CT" *Neurology* 36 (April 1986): 471-88.

Robinson, R.G., Lipsey, J.R., Bolla-Wilson, K., Bolduc, P.L., Pearlson, G.D., Rao, K., and Price, T.R. "Mood Disorders in Left-Handed Stroke Patients" *American Journal of Psychiatry* 142 (December 1985): 1424-29.

Oxygen and Glucose Consumption

Lassen, Niels A.; Ingvar, David H.; and Skinhoj Erik, "Brain Function and Blood Flow" *Scientific American* (October 1978): 62-71.

Other

Carmon, A., and Nachshon, I. "Effect of Unilateral Brain Damage on Perception of Temporal Order" *Cortex* 7 (1971): 410-18.

Deikman, Arthur "Deautomatization and the Mystic Experience" *Psychiatry* 29 (1966): 329-43.

Dimond, Stuart J., and Blizard, David A. *Evolution and Lateralization of the Brain* New York: The New York Academy of Sciences, 1977.

Eccles, Sir John, and Robinson, Daniel N. *The Wonder of Being Human, Our Brain and Our Mind* Boston and London: New Science Library, 1985.

Joseph, R.; Gallagher, R.E.; Holloway, W.; and Kahn, J. "Two Brains, One Child: Interhemispheric Information Transfer Deficits and Confabulatory Responding in Children Aged 4, 7, 10" *Cortex* 20 (September 1984): 317-31.

O'Leary, D.S. "A Developmental Study of Interhemispheric Transfer in Children Aged Five to Ten" *Child Development* 51 (September 1980): 743–50.

Sacks, Oliver W. *The Man Who Mistook His Wife for a Hat and Other Clinical Tales* New York: Summit Books, ca. 1985.

Sillman, L.R. "Four Cardinal Characteristics of Unconscious Mentation" *International Journal of Psychoanalysis* V XXIX Part II (1948): 126ff.

Wells, J.J. "Location for Learning" in *Essays on the Nervous System— A Festschrift for Professor J.Z. Young*, edited by Bellairs, R., and Gray, E.G. (Oxford: Clarendon Press, 1974): 407–30.

Part Two: Psychology

Armstrong, D.M. "Three Types of Consciousness (Commentary)" *Ciba Foundation Symposium* 69 (1979): 235–53.

Austin, M.D. "Dream Recall and the Bias of Intellectual Ability" *Nature* 231 (1971): 59.

Beloff, J. *Psychological Sciences* London: Crosby Lockwood Staples, 1973.

Benson, Herbert *The Relaxation Response* New York: William Morrow, 1975.

Coxhead, David, and Hiller, Susan *Dreams, Visions of the Night* London: Thames and Hudson, ca. 1977.

Ehrlich, E.L. "Der Traum im Alten Testament" *Beihefte zur Zeitschrift für die alttestamentliche Wissenschaft* 72 (Berlin, 1953).

Evans, Christopher *Landscapes of the Night: How and Why We Dream* New York: Viking Press 1983.

Foulkes, David "How Do Hypnagogic Dreams Differ From REM Dreams?" *Psychology of Sleep; Psychological Bulletin* 62 (1964).

———. *The Psychology of Sleep* New York: Scribner's Sons, 1966.

Graham, W.C. *The Prophets and Israel's Culture* Chicago; The University of Chicago Press 1934.

Guillaume, Alfred *Prophecy and Divination Among the Hebrews and other Semites* The Bampton Lectures, New York: Harper & Brothers, 1938.

Haeussermann, F. "Wortempfang und Symbol in der alttestamentlichen Prophetie. Eine Untersuchung zur Psychologie des prophetischen

Erlebnisses." *Beiheft zur Zeitschrift für die alttestamentliche Wissenschaft* 58 (Giessen, 1932).

Hall, Brian P. *The Development of Consciousness, A Confluent Theory of Values* New York: Paulist Press, 1976.

Hoppe, K.D. "Split Brains and Psychoanalysis" *Psychoanalytic Quarterly* 46 (1977): 220–24.

Hoppe, K.D. "Split-brain: Psychoanalytic Findings and Hypotheses" *Journal of the American Academy of Psychoanalysis* 6 (April 1978): 193–213.

Horton, P., and Miller, D. "The Etiology of Multiple Personality" *Comprehensive Psychiatry* 13 (1972): 151–59.

Johnston, William *Silent Music: the Science of Meditation* New York: Harper & Row, 1974.

Kelsey, Morton Trippe *The Other Side of Silence: a Guide to Christian Meditation* New York: Paulist Press, 1976.

Klein, W.C. *The Psychological Pattern of Old Testament Prophecy* Evanston: Seabury-Western Theological Seminary 1956.

Knight, H. *The Hebrew Prophetic Consciousness* London: Lutterworth Press 1947.

LeShan, Lawrence *How to Meditate* New York: Bantam Books, 1975.

_____. *The Medium, the Mystic, and the Physicist* New York: Viking Press, 1974.

Myers, F.W.H. "Automatic Writing" *Proceedings of the Society for Psychical Research* VIII (1885): 1–63.

Naranjo, Claudio, and Ornstein, Robert *On the Psychology of Meditation* New York: Viking Press, 1971.

Oesterreich, T. *Die Besessenheit* Langensalza, 1921.

Ornstein, Robert E. *The Psychology of Consciousness* New York: The Viking Press, 1972.

_____. *The Nature of Human Consciousness* New York: The Viking Press, 1973.

Oswald, Ian "Drowsy Dreams are Micro Dreams" in *The New World of Dreams* edited by Woods, Ralph, and Greenhouse, Herbert B. New York: Macmillan, 1974: 314.

Peacocke, A.R. "Reductionism: A Review of the Epistemological Issues and Their Relevance to Biology and the Problem of Consciousness" *Zygon: Journal of Religion and Science*, 11 (1976): 308.

Povah, J.W. *The New Psychology and the Hebrew Prophets* New York: Longmans, Green 1925.

Schreiber, Flora Rheta *Sybil* New York: Warner Books, 1973.

Sister, Moses "Die Typen der Prophetischen Visionen in der Bibel" *Monatsschrift für Geschichte und Wissenschaft des Judentums* 78 (1934): 399-430.

Tart, Charles T., ed. *Altered States of Consciousness* Garden City, New York: Anchor Books, Doubleday, 1969.

_____. *States of Consciousness* New York: John Wiley and Sons, 1969.

Thigpen, C.H., and Cleckley, H.M. *The Three Faces of Eve* London: Secker and Warburg, 1957.

Van de Castle, Robert L. *The Psychology of Dreaming* Morristown, N.J.: General Learning Corporation, 1971.

Widengren, G. *Literary and Psychological Aspects of the Hebrew Prophets* Uppsala, UUA:10, 1948.

Winson, Jonathan *Brain and Psyche* Garden City: Anchor Press, Doubleday, 1985.

Wolman, Benjamin B., and Ullman, Montague *Handbook of States of Consciousness* New York: Van Nostrand Reinhold, 1986.

Part Three: Parapsychology and Paraphysics

Altom, Kathleen, and Braud, William G. "Clairvoyant and Telepathic Impressions of Musical Targets" in *Research in Parapsychology 1975, Research Briefs (III)*, edited by Morris, Joanna, Roll, W.G., and Morris, R.L. Metuchen, N.J.: Scarecrow Press 1976: 171-74.

Alvarado, Carlos S. "ESP During Out-of-Body Experiences: A Review of Experimental Studies" in *Journal of Parapsychology* 46 (September, 1982): 209-30.

_____. "Phenomenological Aspects of Out-of-Body Experiences: A Report of Three Studies" in *Journal of the American Society for Psychical Research* 78 (July 1984): 219-44.

Andre, Joel, "Je Parle aux Chevaux . . . Ils Me Répondent!" in *Psi, La Grande Revue Internationale du Surnaturel Face à la Science* (Bimestriel Septembre, Octobre, 1977): 90-100.

Barry, Jean "Retarding Fungus Growth by PK" in *Progress in Parapsychology* edited by Rhine, J.B. (Durham, N.C.: The Parapsychology Press, 1971): 118-21.

Blackmore, Susan J. "A Psychological Theory of the Out-of-Body Experience" *Journal of Parapsychology* 48 (September 1984): 201–18.

_____. "Out-of-Body Experiences, Lucid Dreams, and Imagery: Two Surveys" *Journal of the American Society for Psychical Research* 76 (October 1982): 301–18.

Bowles, Norma, and Hynds, Fran, with Maxwell, Joan *Psi Search* New York: Harper and Row, 1978.

Braud, W.G., Smith, G., Andrew, F., and Willis, S. "Psychokinetic Influences on Random Number Generators During Evocation of Analytic' versus 'Non-Analytic' Modes of Processing Information" *Research in Parapsychology* (1975):98–102.

Brier, Robert "PK Effect on a Plant-Polygraph System" in *Progress in Parapsychology* edited by Rhine, J.B. (Durham, N.C.: The Parapsychology Press, 1971): 102–17.

Broughton, Richard S. "Brain Hemisphere Specialization and Its Possible Effects on ESP Performance" *Research in Parapsychology 1975*, (Metuchen, N.J.: Scarecrow Press, 1976): 98–102.

_____. "Possible Brain Hemisphere Laterality Effects in ESP Performance" *Journal of the American Society for Psychical Research* 48 (December 1976): 384–99.

_____. "Psi and the Two Halves of the Brain" *Journal of the American Society for Psychical Research* 48 (September 1975): 140–41.

Carrington, Whatley "Experiments on the Paranormal Cognition of Drawings" *Proceedings of the Society for Psychical Research* 46 (1940): 23–151, 277–334; 47 (1944): 155–228; 24 (1944): 3–107.

Cook, Anne M., and Irwin, Harvey J. "Visuospatial Skills and the Out-of-Body Experience" *Journal of Parapsychology* 47 (March 1983): 23–35.

Deikman, Arthur "Bimodal Consciousness" *Archives of General Psychiatry* 25 (December 1971): 481–89.

Ehrenwald, Jan *Anatomy of Genius, Split Brains and Global Minds* New York: Human Sciences Press, 1984.

_____. "Cerebral Localization and the Psi Syndrome" *Journal of Nervous and Mental Disease* 161 (1975): 393ff.

_____. *The ESP Experience, A Psychiatric Validation* New York: Basic Books, 1978.

_____. *New Dimensions of Deep Analysis: A Study of Telepathy in Interpersonal Relationships* New York: Grune and Stratton, 1966.

_____. "Psi Phenomena, Hemispheric Dominance and the Existential Shift" *Parapsychology Review* 9 (September-October 1978): 1-3.

_____. "Right- vs. Left-Hemispheric Approach in Psychical Research" *Journal of the American Society for Psychical Research* 78 (1984): 29-39.

Eisenbud, Jule *Paranormal Foreknowledge* New York: Human Sciences Press, 1982.

Gertz, John "Hypnagogic Fantasy, EEG, and Psi Performance in a Single Subject" *Journal of the American Society for Psychical Research* 77 (April 1983): 155-170.

Grad, B. "A Telekinetic Effect on Plant Growth, I" *International Journal of Parapsychology* 5 (1963): 117-33.

_____. "A Telekinetic Effect on Plant Growth, II" *International Journal of Parapsychology* 6 (1964): 473-98.

Gross, Michael "Toward an Explanation of Near-Death Phenomena" *Journal of the American Society for Psychical Research* 75 (January 1981): 37-60.

Hasted, John *The Metal Benders* London, Boston: Routledge and Kegan Paul, 1981.

Heaney, John J. *The Sacred and the Psychic, Parapsychology and Christian Theology* Ramsey, N.J.: Paulist Press, 1984.

Holzer, Hans *The Psychic Side of Dreams* New York: Doubleday, 1976.

Honorton, C. "Reported Frequency of Dream Recall and ESP" *Journal of the American Society for Psychical Research* 66 (1972): 369-74.

Horton, P., and Miller, D. "The Etiology of Multiple Personality" *Comprehensive Psychiatry* 13 (1972): 151-59.

Klein, Judith "Lalsingh Harribance, Medium in Residence" *Theta* 31 (Spring 1971).

Koestler, Arthur *The Roots of Coincidence, An Excursion Into Parapsychology* New York: Vintage Books, 1973.

Krieger, Dolores *The Therapeutic Touch: How to Use Your Hands to Help or to Heal* New York: Prentice Hall, 1979.

Locke, Thomas P., and Shontz, Franklin C. "Personality Correlates of the Near-Death Experience: A Preliminary Study" *Journal of the American Society for Psychical Research* 77 (October 1983): 311-18.

Lovitts, Barbara E. "The Sheep-Goat Effect Turned Upside Down" *Journal of Parapsychology* 4 (December 1981).

Luria, A.R. *The Working Brain* New York: Basic Books, 1973.

Maher, Michaeleen "Correlated Hemispheric Asymmetry in the Sensory and ESP Processing of 'Emotional' and 'Nonemotional' Videotapes" New York: Diss. Ph.D. The City University of New York, 1983.

Maher, Michaeleen; Peratsakis, Demetrios; and Schmeidler, Gertrude R. "Cerebral Lateralization Effects in ESP Processing: An Attempted Replication" *Journal of the American Society for Psychical Research* 73 (1979): 167-77.

Maher, Michaeleen, and Schmeidler, Gertrude R. "Cerebral Lateralization Effects in ESP Processing" *Journal of the American Society for Psychical Research* 71 (1977): 261-71.

Martinez-Taboas, Alfonso "An Appraisal of the Role of Aggression and the Central Nervous System in RSPK Agents" *Journal of the American Society for Psychical Research* 78 (January 1984): 55-69.

Meyers, Susan A.; Austrin, Harvey R.; Grisso, J. Thomas; and Nickeson, Richard C. "Personality Characteristics as Related to the Out-of-Body Experience" *Journal of Parapsychology* 47 (June 1982): 131-44.

Monroe, Robert A. *Journeys Out of the Body* New York: Anchor Press/Doubleday, 1971.

Moody, Raymond A., Jr. *Life After Life* New York: Bantam Book, 1975.

————. *Reflections on Life After Life,* New York: Bantam Books, 1977.

Moore, E. Garth *Try the Spirits, Christianity and Psychical Research* New York: Oxford University Press, 1977.

Morris, Robert L. "Assessing Experimental Support for True Precognition" *Journal of Parapsychology* 46 (December 1982): 321-36.

Nash, Carroll B. "Test of Psychokinetic Control of Bacterial Mutation" *The Journal of the American Society for Psychical Research* 78 (April 1984): 145-50.

Omez, Reginald *Psychical Phenomena* New York: Hawthorn Books, 1958.

Osis, Karlis, and McCormick, Donna "A Poltergeist Case Without an Identifiable Living Agent" *Journal of the American Society for Psychical Research* 76 (January 1982): 23–51.

Overholt, Thomas W. *Prophecy in Cross-Cultural Perspective* Atlanta: Scholars Press, 1986.

Panati, Charles *Supersenses, Our Potential for Parasensory Experience, A Survey of Current Knowledge* Garden City, New York: Anchor Books, 1976.

Parker, Adrian *States of Mind: ESP and Altered States of Consciousness* New York: Taplinger, 1975.

Pratt, J. Gaither *Parapsychology, an Insider's View of ESP* London: W.H. Allen, 1964.

Pratt, J. Gaither, and Keil, H.H. "Firsthand Observations of Nina S. Kulagina Suggestive of PK Upon Static Objects" *Journal of the American Society for Psychical Research* (October 1973): 381–90.

Puthoff, H.E., and Targ, R. "A Perceptual Channel for Information Transfer over Kilometer Distances: Historical Perspective and Recent Research" *The Institute of Electrical and Electronics Engineers, Inc.* annals no. 603PR004 (1976): 329–54.

Rhine, Louisa E. *Psi, What Is It?, The Story of ESP and PK* New York: Perennial Library, Harper and Row, 1975.

Richmond, N. "Two Series of PK Tests on Paramecia" *Journal of the American Society for Psychical Research* 36 (1952): 577–88.

Robinson, Diana "ESP Scoring Patterns in Left-handed Subjects" *Parapsychology Review* 8 (January-February 1977): 16–18.

Rogo, D. Scott *Parapsychology: A Century of Inquiry* New York: Dell Publishing, 1975.

Roll, William G., and Montagno, Elson de A. "Neurophysical Aspects of Psi." (Unpublished manuscript, December 1983, Psychical Research Foundation, located at the Parapsychological Foundation, New York).

Rushton, W.A.H. "First Sight—Second Sight" *Proceedings of the Society for Psychical Research* 55 (1971): 177–88.

Salley, Roy D. "REM Sleep Phenomena During Out-of-Body Experiences" *Journal of the American Society for Psychical Research* 76 (April 1982): 157–66.

Schlit, Marilyn J., and Haight, Jo Marie "Remote Viewing Revisited: An Intrasubject Replication" *Journal of Parapsychology* 48 (March 1984): 39-50.

Schmeidler, G.R. "Research Findings in Psychokinesis" in *Advances in Parapsychological Research* Vol. I, *Psychokinesis*, edited by Krippner, Stanley (New York: Plenium Press, 1977).

_____. "PK Effects Upon Continuously Recorded Temperature" *Journal of the American Society for Psychical Research* 67 (October 1973): 325-40.

Schmeidler, G.R., McConnell, R.A. *ESP and Personality Patterns* New Haven, Conn.: Yale University Press, 1958.

Schmidt, H., and Pantas, L. "PK Tests with Internally Different Machines" *Journal of Parapsychology* 36 (1972): 222-32.

Sinclair, Upton *Mental Radio* Springfield, Ill.: Charles C. Thomas, 1962.

Smythies, J.R. *Science and ESP* New York: Humanities Press, 1967.

Stanford, R.G. "An Experimentally Testable Model for Spontaneous Psi Events, I Extrasensory Events" *Journal of the American Society for Psychical Research* 68 (1974a): 34-57.

_____. "An Experimentally Testable Model for Spontaneous Psi Events, II Psychokinetic Events" *Journal of the American Society for Psychical Research* 68 (1974b): 321-56.

Stanford, R.G., and Lovin, C. "EEG Alpha Activity and ESP Performance" *Journal of the American Society for Psychical Research* 64 (1970): 375-84.

Swann, Ingo *To Kiss Earth Goodbye* New York: Hawthorn Books, 1975.

Targ, Russell, and Morris, Robert L. "Note on a Reanalysis of the UCSB Remote-Viewing Experiments" *Journal of Parapsychology* 46 (March 1982): 47-50.

Thalbourne, Michael A. "Extraversion and the Sheep-Goat Variable: A Conceptual Replication" *Journal of the American Society for Psychical Research* 75 (April 1981): 105-20.

Tocquet, Robert "Les Expériences que J'ai Réalisées avec J.P. Girard" in *Psi, La Grande Revue Internationale du Surnaturel Face à la Science* (Bimestriel Septembre-Octobre 1977): 20-25.

Ullman, Montague; Krippner, Stanley; and Vaughan, A. *Dream Telepathy* New York: Macmillan, 1973.

Zaehner, R.C. *Mysticism Sacred and Profane; An Inquiry into Some Varieties of Praeternatural Experience* Oxford 1957.

Part Four: The Study of Biblical Literature

Blenkinsopp, Joseph *A History of Prophecy in Israel* Philadelphia: Westminster Press, 1983.

Broome, E.C. "Ezekiel's Abnormal Personality" *Journal of Biblical Literature* 65 (1946): 277ff.

Burridge, Kenelm O.L. "Reflections on Prophecy and Prophetic Groups" Chico, Cal., Scholars' Press 1982 *Semeia* 21: 99–102.

Buss, Maartin J. "An Anthropological Perspective Upon Prophetic Call Narratives" Chico, Cal., Scholars' Press 1982 *Semeia* 21: 9–30.

Caird, G.B. *The Revelation of St. John the Divine* Black's New Testament Commentaries, London: A. & C. Black, 1984.

Carroll, Robert P. *When Prophecy Failed: Cognitive Dissonance in the Prophetic Traditions of the Old Testament* New York: Seabury, 1979.

Chisholm, Robert B., Jr. "Wordplay in the Eighth-Century Prophets" *Bibliotheca Sacra* 144 (January-March 1987): 44–52.

Clements, R.E. "The Ezekiel Tradition: Prophecy in a Time of Crisis" in *Israel's Prophetic Tradition* edited by Coggins, Richard, et al. (Cambridge: Cambridge University Press 1982): 119–36.

Collins, John J. *The Apocalyptic Vision of the Book of Daniel* Missoula, Mont.: Scholars Press for Harvard Semitic Museum, 1977.

Efird, James M. *Daniel and Revelation, A Study of Two Extraordinary Visions* Valley Forge: Judson Press, 1978.

Ford, J. Massyngberde "Revelation: Introduction, Translation and Commentary" *The Anchor Bible*, Garden City, New York: Doubleday & Company, 1975.

Greenberg, Moshe "On Ezekiel's Dumbness" *Journal of Biblical Literature* 77 (1958): 101–05.

Gunnel, Andre "Ecstatic Prophecy in the Old Testament" in *Religious Ecstasy* edited by Holm, N.G., Scripta Instituti Donneriani Aboensis 11 (1982): 187–200.

Hammer, Raymond "The Book of Daniel," *The Cambridge Bible Commentary* New York: Cambridge University Press, 1976.

Hartman, Louis F. "The Book of Daniel" in *The Anchor Bible* Garden City, New York: Doubleday, 1977.

Hobbs, T.R. "The Search for Prophetic Consciousness; Comments on Method" *Biblical Theology Bulletin* t15 (1985): 136–41.

Kepler, Thomas S. *Dreams of the Future, Daniel and Revelation* New York: Abingdon Press, 1963.

Knibb, Michael A. "Prophecy and the Emergence of Jewish Apocalypses" in *Israel's Prophetic Tradition* edited by Coggins, Richard, et al (New York: Cambridge University Press, 1982): 155–80.

Knight, Harold "The Personality of Ezekiel: Priest or Prophet?" *Expository Times*, 61 (1943): 115ff.

Lacocque, André *The Book of Daniel* Atlanta: John Knox Press, 1979.

Lindblom, J. *Prophecy in Ancient Israel* Philadelphia: Fortress Press, 1963.

McKane, W. "Prophecy and the Prophetic Literature" in *Tradition and Interpretation*, edited by Anderson, G.W. (Oxford: Oxford University Press): 163–88.

Mendelsohn, I. "dream, dreamer" in *Interpreter's Dictionary of the Bible* Nashville: Abingdon, 1962.

Napier, B.D. "Vision" *Interpreter's Dictionary of the Bible* Nashville: Abingdon, 1962.

Niditch, Susan "The Symbolic Vision in Biblical Tradition" *Harvard Semitic Monographs 30* XII (Chico, Cal.: Scholars' Press, 1983): 1–258.

Overholt, Thomas W. *Prophecy in Cross-Cultural Perspective, A Sourcebook for Biblical Researchers* Atlanta, Georgia: Scholars' Press, 1986.

Parker, Simon B. "Possession Trance and Prophecy in Pre-Exilic Israel" *Vetus Testamentum* 28 (1978): 271–85.

Porteous, Norman W. *Daniel, A Commentary* London: SCM Press Ltd., 1965.

Ringgren, Helmer "Prophecy in the Ancient Near East" in *Israel's Prophetic Tradition* edited by Coggins, Richard, et al. (Cambridge: Cambridge University Press, 1982): 1–11.

Robinson, H. Wheeler *Inspiration and Revelation in the Old Testament* Oxford: Clarendon Press, 1946.

Sawyer, John F. A. "A Change of Emphasis in the Study of the Prophets" in *Israel's Prophetic Tradition,* edited by Coggins, Richard et al. (Cambridge: Cambridge University Press, 1982): 233–49.

Van Nuys, Kelvin "Evaluating the Pathological in Prophetic Experience (Particularly in Ezekiel)" *Journal of Bible and Religion,* 21 (1953): 244–51.

Wilson, Robert R. "Prophecy and Ecstasy: A Reexamination" *Journal of Biblical Literature* 98 (1979): 321–37.

Zimmerli, Walther "Visionary Experiences in Jeremiah" in *Israel's Prophetic Tradition* edited by Coggins, Richard et al (Cambridge: Cambridge University Press, 1982): 95–118.